SELECTED POEMS

Edna St. Vincent Millay

SELECTED POEMS

The Centenary Edition

Edited and with an introduction
by Colin Falck

HarperPerennial
A Division of HarperCollins*Publishers*

Designed by Cassandra J. Pappas

The Library of Congress has catalogued the hardcover edition as follows:

Millay, Edna St. Vincent, 1892–1950.
    [Poems. Selections]
    Selected poems of Edna St. Vincent Millay : the centenary edition
    edited by Colin Falck.—1st ed.
      p.   cm.
    Includes index.
    ISBN 0-06-016733-5
    I. Falck, Colin.   II. Title.
    PS3525.I495A6   1991   91-55102
811'.52—dc20

ISBN 0-06-092288-5 (pbk.)

93 94 95 96 AC/CW 10 9 8 7 6 5 4 3

CONTENTS

FROM *SECOND APRIL* (1921)

FROM *THE HARP-WEAVER AND OTHER POEMS* (1923)

FROM *HUNTSMAN, WHAT QUARRY?* (1939)

FROM *MINE THE HARVEST* (1954)

FOREWORD

I CAME UP from the Library of Congress to Steepletop in Auster-
litz, New York, to Edna Millay's place. Her sister and her sister's
husband were there. The place gave off an aroma of her spirit. I
was invited to go down into the cellar. There were still several
bottles of wine in a row on a shelf which had been laid down by
Vincent (as Millay was known to her close friends) and her hus-
band, who had long ago ordered a carload of grapes to be sent
from California. We savored a wine like Spring. I brought some
back to Washington. I also secured two of the poet's dresses and
two pairs of shoes, and took them back to Washington as well.
My wife, Betty, decided which to give where—one to the Library
of Congress, one to the Museum of American History. At the
latter, a mannequin, life-sized among many such, was dressed in
Vincent's clothes, and gave a startling sense of reality. The whole
display was of great women of America.

I remember how, when I was at Millay's house, she had
been said occasionally to sit on the third step of the staircase that
went up to the second floor. I would pause and envision her there.
Upstairs was a small library room, and the first time I was in it
I had been awed to find on her shelves a copy of an early book of
my own poetry.

Had I not heard her read in a red dress in the afternoon in

Robinson Hall at Dartmouth when I was an undergraduate? And had I not been enraptured as I followed her back to the Inn, lagging a hundred feet behind her, anonymous, afraid to go up and say hello or to touch her? I was not only enraptured but afraid of the greatness of poetry. I worshipped Millay as a possessor of immortality. She was too beautiful to live among mortals. She symbolized Platonic beauty.

Richard Eberhart

ABOUT THE AUTHOR

EDNA ST. VINCENT MILLAY WAS BORN in 1892 in Rockland, Maine, the eldest of three daughters, and was encouraged by her mother to develop her talents for music and poetry. Her long poem "Renascence" won critical attention in an anthology contest in 1912 and secured for her a patron who enabled her to go to Vassar College. After graduating in 1917 she lived in Greenwich Village in New York for a few years, acting, writing satirical pieces for journals (usually under a pseudonym), and continuing to work at her poetry. She traveled in Europe throughout 1921–22 as a "foreign correspondent" for *Vanity Fair*. Her collection *A Few Figs from Thistles* (1920) gained her a reputation for hedonistic wit and cynicism, but her other collections (including the earlier *Renascence and Other Poems* [1917]) are without exception more seriously passionate or reflective. In 1923 she married Eugen Boissevain and—after further travel—embarked on a series of reading tours which helped to consolidate her nationwide renown. From 1925 onwards she lived at Steepletop, a farmstead in Austerlitz, New York, where her husband protected her from all responsibilities except her creative work. Often involved in feminist or political causes (including the Sacco-Vanzetti case of 1927), she turned to writing anti-fascist propaganda poetry in 1940 and further damaged a reputation already in decline before changed fashions. In her last years her life became more withdrawn and isolated, and her health, which had never been robust, became increasingly poor. She died in 1950. Her posthumous collection *Mine the Harvest* (1954) contains some of her most technically original work.

INTRODUCTION:

The Modern Lyricism
of Edna Millay

THE POETRY OF Edna St. Vincent Millay combines spiritual intensity with intellectual sophistication in a way which may constitute an almost unimaginable unity of sensibility for present-day readers. Rejected by "modernist" critics as sentimental in her concerns and unreconstructedly nineteenth-century in her methods, Millay has in the years since her death become the captive of her least poetically-educated admirers; yet it seems likely that it is a fear of the very simplicity of her poetry—and of the challenge that it poses to us to experience life with something of the intensity with which earlier, and less ironic, generations experienced it—that mainly lies behind her neglect by today's highbrow readership.

Millay's work has lost its representation in many of the more serious anthologies throughout recent decades, even though her poetry has at no time been out of print since the first publication of her *Collected Poems* in 1956. One of the more significant of such omissions is from *The New Oxford Book of American Verse,* edited by Richard Ellmann, of 1976 (F. O. Matthiessen had included several of Millay's poems in his *Oxford Book of American*

Verse of 1950). Geoffrey Moore, in his *Penguin Book of American Verse* of 1977, gives space to two of Millay's sonnets but can find nothing to say about her work or her significance in his long and detailed introductory essay. Millay is no longer a part of any trend or tendency that is seen as having helped to make American poetry what it is today (in which perception there is perhaps a good deal of ironic truth), and her distinctive achievement, like that of any poet whose work relies on lyrical directness or firmness of tone, is almost entirely incapable of being discussed within the reflexive and involuted terms of present-day critical debate. Yet as the early-twentieth-century smoke continues to clear, and as it becomes evident how far the appeals of irony may have helped to de-sensitize us to the more elemental or primitive energies of life itself, it has begun to be possible to look at certain parts of the modern tradition afresh. It has begun to be possible to see that certain very important poets have been entirely written out of the tradition—Robinson Jeffers is an example—because of their refusal to embrace the central tenets of modernism. It may even have begun to be possible to see that Edna Millay was the finest American lyricist of the twentieth century, and that in her mastery of the older forms as well as in her unique development of the Whitmanian tradition of cadenced free verse (in which she was chiefly influenced by Jeffers), she was one of the most skillful technicians in the whole history of English poetry.

One of the most striking things about Millay's sensibility is that irony was always a deep need of her nature—and yet that she never at any time succumbed to the temptation to allow it to become the deepest need of all. Her satirical intelligence was as sharp as Robinson's or Frost's or Eliot's, and her wit—as in her letters and in her Greenwich Village-period writings for such journals as *Vanity Fair*—often as mercurial as Wilde's; yet her deepest instinct was always to pass through and beyond such left-handed engagements with the times she lived in and to address herself to the more essential, and essentially tragic, truths of human existence. Transcending life's ironies rather than merely taking her stand in them, she reached towards what Blake might have seen as a radical innocence on the far side of our twentieth-century experience. Few poets—and they include Hardy and Housman, whom Millay admired, and who admired her in return—have succeeded in holding together irony and lyricism within the same deeply unified vision of life. As clear-eyed and religiously unillusioned as writers such as these, Millay embodies in much of her work the lyric stoicism of a poem like Hardy's "During Wind and Rain," while at the same time being ready to immerse herself in the detailed sufferings and tribulations of human beings (not least of women) within modern social circumstances and to locate these within her overall perspective. There is something distinctively twentieth-century about such a project (although it has one of its sources in such nineteenth-century poetry as Meredith's *Modern Love*), and it may eventually come to be seen as one of the ways in which twentieth-century poetry established its continuity with the past—rather than, for example, using the nobler past as a stick to beat the degraded present with—and thereby acquired its power to point towards a poetic future. Allen Tate, one of the few modernist critics to have sensed Millay's significance at the time when she was writing, called her "the one poet of our time who has successfully stood athwart two ages."

A considerable part of Millay's writing, even so—and she was perhaps too precocious and too willful ever to have adequately deconstructed her own shortcomings—is indeed marred by the kinds of naive-seeming traditionalism for which modernists have berated her. Apostrophes and exclamations, stylized lyric posturings, cutely traditional elisions, poetical inversions of grammar and word-order, personifications of love or death or beauty, nursery-rhyme metrics, slightly-too-facile epigrams, more-than-slightly-too-facile metaphors or symbols, all leap from the page for the casual reader of Millay's *Collected Lyrics* or *Collected Sonnets*. Millay sometimes seems to have felt a perverse affection for these outmoded poeticisms, almost as though they were endangered species which needed her protection. There is no denying, as James Gray has pointed out in a sympathetic critique, that

> [t]he familiar image, drawn from the treasury of metaphor upon which Shakespeare also depended for imaginative resource, seems never to have dismayed her. . . . For her, death still swung his scythe and the poems in which he does so with the old familiar ruthlessness betray no nervous apprehension that the instrument may have become rusty or blunted with the use of ages.

Yet against all this must be set the substantial proportion of Millay's work—about a quarter, perhaps—which is entirely twentieth-century in its manner and poetic implications and which is sufficient on its own to entitle her to consideration as one of the major poets of the century. If we add to such essential modernity her more individually distinctive qualities—her astonishing yet unobtrusive brilliance with English syntax, her complex and extremely subtle feminist consciousness, her almost Blakean sense of the mysteriousness of ordinary life—she becomes a poet of unusual power and significance for readers today. Consider, for example, the closing lines of "Men Working," a poem of the 1940s (a period which had seen, or was seeing, the collapse of almost every imaginable kind of facile poetic heroism):

> The clean strike of the pike into the pole; each man
> Depending on the skill
> And the balance, both of body and of mind,
> Of each of the others: in the back of each man's mind

The respect for the pole: it is forty feet high, and weighs
Two thousand pounds.

In the front of each man's mind: "She's going to go
Exactly where we want her to go: this pole
Is going to go into that seven-foot hole we dug
For her
To stand in."

This was in the deepening dusk of a July night.
They were putting in the poles: bringing the electric light.

Or the concrete detail of this opening sonnet from a long domestic sequence:

So she came back into his house again
And watched beside his bed until he died,
Loving him not at all. The winter rain
Splashed on the painted butter-tub outside,
Where once her red geraniums had stood,
Where still their rotted stalks were to be seen;
The thin log snapped; and she went out for wood,
Bareheaded, running the few steps between
The house and shed; there, from the sodden eaves
Blown back and forth on ragged ends of twine,
Saw the dejected creeping-jinny vine,
(And one, big-aproned, blithe, with stiff blue sleeves
Rolled to the shoulder that warm day in spring,
Who planted seeds, musing ahead to their far blossoming).

Or the verse-movement *tour de force* of this final section of the five-part poem "Tristan":

Heavily on the faithful bulk of Kurvenal,
My servant for a long time, leaning,

With footsteps less from weakness than for pleasure in the
    green grass, lagging, I came here,
Out of the house, to lie, propped up on pillows, under this
    fine tree—
Oak older than I, but still, not being ill, growing,
Granted to feel, I think, barring lightning, year after
    year,—and barring the axe—
For a long time yet, the green sap flowing.

These are achievements of a poet who has lived with, chosen
among, and made her own contributions to the great poetic
advances of the early twentieth century. They should bring joy to
the hearts of even the most hard-bitten of modernist-minded
readers.

A world-embracing intensity and a world-repudiating scorn
were co-present in Millay's vision from the start, and the preco-
cious nineteen-year-old Maine girl who made her name with
"Renascence" and the style-conscious Greenwich Village ironist
of only a few years later were one and the same individual. There
is no incompatibility, and scarcely a very dramatic transition,
between the final lines of "Renascence"—

But East and West will pinch the heart
That can not keep them pushed apart;
And he whose soul is flat—the sky
Will cave in on him by and by

—and the advice which Millay (under her pseudonym Nancy
Boyd) gave to an imaginary Greenwich Village correspondent
worried about her inability to attract a sufficient number of as-
piring artists to her apartment:

The trouble is with the ashtrays; remove them. Get into the
habit when alone of crushing out your cigarette against the

wall-paper, or dropping it on the floor and carelessly grinding it into the rug, or tossing it in the general direction of the fire-place, if you have one, being very sure never to look anxiously after it to see where it lands. This easy manner on your part will do more than anything else to put your guests at ease. Soon they will be using your studio as if it were their own, going to sleep with their feet in the coffee-tray, wiping paint from their hair and elbows upon the sofa-pillows, making sketches on the walls of unclothed people with small heads and over-developed muscles, and dropping ashes just everywhere.

What links these very different kinds of exhortation together is poetic passion and a fierce contempt for all the prevailing forms of inauthentic living. Millay is less well understood as a backward-looking sentimentalist than as a lyric-ironist in a tradition which (in addition to Blake and Emily Dickinson) includes the later French Symbolists, Wilde, Hardy, Housman, and the younger Eliot, as well as many of the existentialist prose writers of the later nineteenth and earlier twentieth centuries. If she sometimes seems too much the mere epigrammatist, on the other hand—as in her 1920 ("My candle burns at both ends") volume, which led many commentators later to bracket her with Dorothy Parker—much the same criticism has commonly been made of T. S. Eliot in the volume which he brought out in that same year. Both poets were caught up in the conflicts of a romanticism at odds with the modern world, and both were trying to find their way towards deeper spiritual solutions.

The existential fierceness with which Millay rejected—on behalf of herself, of all women, of all people—society's offered roles is expressed in poem after poem and is a central preoccupation of her earlier work. She could give this wildness a brilliant and disturbing comic turn, as in "My candle burns at both ends," or in its less famous companion-epigram—

> Safe upon the solid rock the ugly houses stand:
> Come and see my shining palace built upon the sand!

—but the twentiesish precariousness of such spiritual integrity (neatly caught in this epigram's emotional ambiguity) is never entirely distinguishable from nervous desperation or exhaustion. Unlike for example Robert Frost, the earlier Millay could never bring herself to weigh up and to pronounce upon the conflict between security and exposure—Frost's principal theme, and what makes him seem, and mostly be, a wiser poet—but always projected herself as the priestess, and at the same time the sacrificial victim, of the choice of exposure. Wisdom was not her concern (although she later came to express a considerable amount of it); instead, she gives us an unworldly fervor and a refusal to compromise with the available worldly interpretations of life's meanings. (In this respect she has more in common with writers like Dostoevsky or Kafka than with the American women poets with whom she is usually compared.) In the more serious and less epigrammatical of her early poems there is no fulfillment to be found in the world of ordinarily-breathing human passion:

> Tiresome heart, forever living and dying,
> House without air, I leave you and lock your door.
> Wild swans, come over the town, come over
> The town again, trailing your legs and crying!

A mysterious, once-heard voice can haunt us to the very end of what we think of as our lives:

> Earth now
> On the busy brow.
> And where is the voice that I heard crying?

Trains can beguile us from our sleep and from our daily commitments—"there isn't a train I wouldn't take, / No matter where it's going"—and the sea continually calls to us with messages both of liberation and extinction. All of these are the powerful and unsettling apprehensions of a poet for whom life's normal options are little more than options in claustrophobia: a poet who is ultimately homeless.

Millay's refusal to accept the actualities of life as they conventionally come to us can extend to an almost-philosophical arraignment of the physical body itself. In this she commits herself to a notion (it is a philosophical illusion, in fact) of the essential separateness of mind and body, and makes a resigned and scornful poetry out of it. At other times, and more penetratingly, she recognizes that the war between body and soul that afflicts her is really not a metaphysical necessity but a war between a woman's spiritual independence and the roles that society, and especially men, have insisted on casting her in. Many of her poems explore this theme with great intelligence, and what may superficially look like the celebration or indulgence of flightiness (a notion of Millay and of her work which has dogged her reputation for half a century) is invariably some form of repudiation of the conventionally institutionalized subjection of women. Women *may* at times be witless, but there are reasons why they have come to be so, and there are other reasons why they may choose to go on acting so. In a sonnet such as "I think I should have loved you presently" Millay both embraces, and also goes beyond, the classic feminist analyses of writers such as Wollstonecraft and Mill—and it is no surprise that she was willing to stand up and be counted as a militantly political feminist at many points throughout her life. She goes beyond them, because she was unwilling ever to repudiate or to down-value the power and intensity of heterosexual love. She tried instead to write about the realities of such love; and what may sometimes come across to us as yet more poetry in the tradition of

"No love endures" is very often a poetry that goes as deeply as poetry itself ever can into the question of *why* no love endures. (One recent critic has noticed that Millay's poetic personality is often a *persona*—that she can be a clever "female female impersonator"—but seems not to notice, or perhaps not to care, that such a *persona,* given her attractiveness to men and much else, may have been Millay's shortest poetic road to authenticity and to the depths of the human soul.) Here Millay's preoccupations come close to those of D. H. Lawrence, and her insights are no less perceptive or persuasive than his. What sets Millay apart from—and above—much present-day feminist theorizing and the more aggressive kinds of feminist poetry is that she is able to experience and to present love, both in its initial impulse and in its essential nature, as a passionate surrender. The question is where, in a better world, such a surrender might take us to.

It would not take us into conventional bourgeois marriage; and yet Millay is also—and it is perhaps one of her most important limitations—unable to envisage in her poetry any other form of embodied and enduring relationship that is both spiritual and physical. By the absolute standards of her existentialist notions of integrity this was perhaps inevitable: the ordinary realities of friendship or comradeship were familiar enough to Millay in her life, but they continued to remain beneath the attention of her poetry. (In her own life, marriage seems for Millay to have been a way of retaining her freedom, and her selfless and forbearing husband made it as possible as it ever could have been for her to go on being the unrestricted poet she had been before she married.) Yet there must also have been other reasons, more deeply rooted than poetry or even thought itself, which kept Millay from moving beyond love as intensity to love as mature commitment; and the ultimate consequence of these reasons is that there is a noticeable weakness of content in the middle region of her poetry as it outgrows the limitations of its youth. (Edmund Wilson, who had known her well, remarked of her later years that "she was now back in a rural isolation like her own childhood—but had no children to force her to outgrow her own childhood.") This weakness is more than compensated for by the poems of her final period, but one may nevertheless be surprised, in reading through her work as a whole, how easily the poems of personal pain or of existential freedom are interwoven with, and give way to, the later poems of more generalized philosophical reflection. There is early Millay and there is late Millay, and there is a good deal of overlap between them, but there is very little that could easily be distinguished as the Millay of a "middle period."

In her later volumes Millay emerges as a truly philosophical poet, and her preoccupations with nature, with death, and with the nobilities and shortcomings of human aspirations are expressed in a range of intellectually substantial and technically widely varying poems. Yet even where she is being overtly thoughtful, Millay's method is nearly always to base her poems in concrete and sharply observational detail, and in her meditative sonnet sequence "Epitaph for the Race of Man" (some parts of which she seems to have been working on as early as 1920) the human story is brought to philosophical life through a series of vividly realized quasi-mythic episodes. (The sonnets are loosely Petrarchan in form, and therefore avoid the intellectual temptations of the clinching final couplet.) In her reflections on death, Millay is unable to attain to any state which might be seen as one of renunciation or resignation (and is scarcely unusual in this, even among poets), but comes close to it on a few occasions, as in "From a Train Window":

> Precious
> In the early light, reassuring
> Is the grave-scarred hillside.
> As if after all, the earth might know what it is about.

More often her vision is stoic and Hardyish, and she acknowledges the reality of death both for herself and for others, but without acceptance: "I shall die, but that is all that I shall do for Death"; "I am not resigned." Millay's own health was never robust, but in her final years—after a war-time period in which she had (as she herself felt) debased her talent for propaganda purposes, after the death of her mother and other personal crises, after much battling with alcohol, drugs, and sickness—she recentered herself in her talent and wrote some of her most imaginatively ambitious and technically accomplished poems. Her own life by this time had little left from which she could draw strength, but her commitment to life in her poetry was as strong as ever—and perhaps rather stronger than it had been in the more showily existentialist affirmations of her youth.

As we judge her now, we must judge Millay essentially as a lyricist. But we must also see that she is a lyricist who is capable of incorporating a wide-ranging, sophisticated, and philosophically profound kind of thought into her emotional apprehensions. Her superb intelligence was always more effectively expressed through the lyricist's flash of insight than through any kind of weightier lucubration. Where she uses a form as intellectually pointed as the Shakespearian sonnet (and some of her Shakespearian sonnets, such as "Pity me not because the light of day," or "Now by the path I climbed, I journey back," are surely among the best poems in this form in the language), it is usually the imagery in the earlier part of the poem that does most of the work, to make way for a restrained and quietly inevitable conclusion. Others of her sonnets tread a harder path and avoid intellectuality altogether, while others yet again rely on modernly concrete detail to express their meaning and (since they ignore the conventional sonnet's subdivisions) should probably be seen as flawlessly rhymed and metered descriptive poems rather than as sonnets in the strict sense. The lyricist's flash of insight as a principal means to the revelation of deeper meanings (it amounts, in effect, to a recognition of the "immanence" of the "transcendent") is probably still too untraditional a conception for us yet to have recognized it as one of modern poetry's central methods. Many of Millay's most powerful lines, and several of her most powerful poems, achieve their effect in a way that leaves very little for the reader or critic to gain by means of detailed interpretation (William Empson already notes this as a fundamental quality of poetry and as its most important "type of ambiguity" in *Seven Types of Ambiguity*). Consider, for example, the powerfully atmospheric final lines of Millay's "Winter Night":

> The day has gone in hewing and felling,
> Sawing and drawing wood to the dwelling
> For the night of talk and story-telling.
>
> . . . .
> Here are question and reply,
> And the fire reflected in the thinking eye.
> So peace, and let the bob-cat cry.

Much could be said about this "thinking eye" and this "bob-cat," but we are surely here dealing with a case where there are unlimitedly many "reasons" which, in Empson's words, "combine to give the line[s their] beauty," where the meaning is "hardly in reach of the analyst at all," and where many pages of discussion might fail to take us nearer to an understanding of how the mysteriously resonant final line of the poem really works. This is Millay's method over and over, and it may account for the fact that perhaps more than any other modern poet she has remained popular among such people as still read poetry while continuing to elude systematic analysis and most of those who practice it.

A felt obligation to concreteness, and an awareness that the meaning is in the detail, may also provide the best rationale and justification for Millay's exploratory free verse. In her later poems, she becomes a spectacularly innovative, as well as merely a traditionally consummate (her skill with the caesura would merit a long discussion of its own) verse technician. To the Whitmanian heritage of cadenced free verse she brings the greater reflective tightness of Robinson Jeffers (among the few icons in Millay's personal library is a framed photograph of Jeffers, her near-contemporary) and—still working with long lines—the kind of rhyming and sound-patterning which had so far only rarely been used in free verse (as, for example, by Pound and Eliot—who were, however, usually more interested in end- than in internal rhyming). The result is a formidable combination, and uniquely Millay's. The closing lines of "New England Spring, 1942" are one of its best exemplifications:

> But Spring is wise. Pale and with gentle eyes, one day
>   somewhat she advances;
> The next, with a flurry of snow into flake-filled skies re-
>   treats before the heat in our eyes, and the thing de-
>   signed
> By the sick and longing mind in its lonely fancies—
> The sally which would force her and take her.
> And Spring is kind.
> Should she come running headlong in a wind-whipped acre
> Of daffodil skirts down the mountain into this dark valley
>   we would go blind.

Nothing like this exists anywhere else in English poetry, unless it be in others of Millay's later poems. The meaning of the lines is carried as much by the rhythmic hesitations, the subtly insistent internal-rhyme structure and the skillfully judged punctuation as by the usual poetic devices which are familiar to us in explicatory analysis. This is perhaps a still-unclosed chapter in modern versification.

Millay is a poet who has been buried twice over: once by the generation that needed to get modernism established, and a second time by the academically-inclined critics who have interested themselves only in poetry which presents verbal and intellectual complexities that can be discussed in professional articles or in the seminar room. Millay is to an almost embarrassing degree (though we should ask who it is that ought to be embarrassed) not that kind of poet. But she has also been badly misrepresented by those critics who have gone to the trouble of finding reasons for rejecting her work. Her use of traditional forms, for example, is often deceptive: for all the poems where she seems to fall into pastiche (as in some of her sonnets, or some of her Housmanish early quatrains), there are others where she is engaged in something rather more subtle. The interplay between the grand manner and the artless-conversational is essential to much of her work (it first shows itself in "Renascence"), and it enables her, as it also did later poets like Auden or Philip Larkin, to give the traditional forms a new lease of credibility. Sometimes her use of the grand manner seems almost designed to subvert itself: the sonnet "Whereas at morning in a jeweled crown," about a turbulent contemporary relationship, could seem almost "post-modernist" in the way it clears the air of the very poetic devices it uses:

> Whereas at morning in a jeweled crown
> I bit my fingers and was hard to please,
> Having shook disaster till the fruit fell down
> I feel tonight more happy and at ease:
> Feet running in the corridors, men quick-
> Buckling their sword-belts bumping down the stair,
> Challenge, and rattling bridge-chain, and the click
> Of hooves on pavement—this will clear the air.

There will perhaps always be those who see Millay's poetry as too simple, too sensuous, too passionate, too old-fashioned, too New

England, too un-urban, too un-intellectual, too narrow-ranged, too lightweight, or just too straightforwardly comprehensible, but this can hardly justify the depths of neglect into which her work has been allowed to fall during the past forty years or so. The occulting of Millay's reputation has been one of the literary scandals of the twentieth century, and it is time we found a proper place for this intense, thoughtful, and magnificently literate poet.

I would like to thank Elizabeth Barnett (literary executor for the estate of Edna St. Vincent Millay), Michael Donaghy, Stephanie Koven, Alexis Lykiard, Eva Salzman, and Robert Stein for their help in the preparation of this edition.

C.F.

FROM
RENASCENCE
(1 9 1 7)

And reaching up my hand to try,
I screamed, to feel it touch the sky.

I screamed, and—lo!—Infinity
Came down and settled over me;
Forced back my scream into my chest;
Bent back my arm upon my breast;
And, pressing of the Undefined
The definition on my mind,
Held up before my eyes a glass
Through which my shrinking sight did pass
Until it seemed I must behold
Immensity made manifold;
Whispered to me a word whose sound
Deafened the air for worlds around,
And brought unmuffled to my ears
The gossiping of friendly spheres,
The creaking of the tented sky,
The ticking of Eternity.

I saw and heard, and knew at last
The How and Why of all things, past,
And present, and forevermore.
The Universe, cleft to the core,
Lay open to my probing sense,
That, sickening, I would fain pluck thence
But could not,—nay! but needs must suck
At the great wound, and could not pluck
My lips away till I had drawn
All venom out.—Ah, fearful pawn:
For my omniscience paid I toll

In infinite remorse of soul.
All sin was of my sinning, all
Atoning mine, and mine the gall
Of all regret. Mine was the weight
Of every brooded wrong, the hate
That stood behind each envious thrust,
Mine every greed, mine every lust.

And all the while, for every grief,
Each suffering, I craved relief
With individual desire;
Craved all in vain! And felt fierce fire
About a thousand people crawl;
Perished with each,—then mourned for all!

A man was starving in Capri;
He moved his eyes and looked at me;
I felt his gaze, I heard his moan,
And knew his hunger as my own.
I saw at sea a great fog bank
Between two ships that struck and sank;
A thousand screams the heavens smote;
And every scream tore through my throat.

No hurt I did not feel, no death
That was not mine; mine each last breath
That, crying, met an answering cry
From the compassion that was I.
All suffering mine, and mine its rod;
Mine, pity like the pity of God.

Ah, awful weight! Infinity
Pressed down upon the finite Me!
My anguished spirit, like a bird,
Beating against my lips I heard;
Yet lay the weight so close about
There was no room for it without.
And so beneath the weight lay I
And suffered death, but could not die.

Long had I lain thus, craving death,
When quietly the earth beneath
Gave way, and inch by inch, so great
At last had grown the crushing weight,
Into the earth I sank till I
Full six feet under ground did lie,
And sank no more,—there is no weight
Can follow here, however great.
From off my breast I felt it roll,
And as it went my tortured soul
Burst forth and fled in such a gust
That all about me swirled the dust.

Deep in the earth I rested now.
Cool is its hand upon the brow
And soft its breast beneath the head
Of one who is so gladly dead.
And all at once, and over all
The pitying rain began to fall;
I lay and heard each pattering hoof
Upon my lowly, thatchèd roof,
And seemed to love the sound far more

Than ever I had done before.
For rain it hath a friendly sound
To one who's six feet under ground;
And scarce the friendly voice or face,
A grave is such a quiet place.

The rain, I said, is kind to come
And speak to me in my new home.
I would I were alive again
To kiss the fingers of the rain,
To drink into my eyes the shine
Of every slanting silver line,
To catch the freshened, fragrant breeze
From drenched and dripping apple-trees.
For soon the shower will be done,
And then the broad face of the sun
Will laugh above the rain-soaked earth
Until the world with answering mirth
Shakes joyously, and each round drop
Rolls, twinkling, from its grass-blade top
How can I bear it, buried here,
While overhead the sky grows clear
And blue again after the storm?
O, multi-coloured, multi-form,
Belovèd beauty over me,
That I shall never, never see
Again! Spring-silver, autumn-gold,
That I shall never more behold!—
Sleeping your myriad magic through,
Close-sepulchred away from you!
O God, I cried, give me new birth,

And put me back upon the earth!
Upset each cloud's gigantic gourd
And let the heavy rain, down-poured
In one big torrent, set me free,
Washing my grave away from me!

I ceased; and through the breathless hush
That answered me, the far-off rush
Of herald wings came whispering
Like music down the vibrant string
Of my ascending prayer, and—crash!
Before the wild wind's whistling lash
The startled storm-clouds reared on high
And plunged in terror down the sky!
And the big rain in one black wave
Fell from the sky and struck my grave.

I know not how such things can be;
I only know there came to me
A fragrance such as never clings
To aught save happy living things;
A sound as of some joyous elf
Singing sweet songs to please himself,
And, through and over everything,
A sense of glad awakening.
The grass, a-tiptoe at my ear,
Whispering to me I could hear;
I felt the rain's cool finger-tips
Brushed tenderly across my lips,
Laid gently on my sealèd sight,
And all at once the heavy night

Fell from my eyes and I could see!—
A drenched and dripping apple-tree,
A last long line of silver rain,
A sky grown clear and blue again.
And as I looked a quickening gust
Of wind blew up to me and thrust
Into my face a miracle
Of orchard-breath, and with the smell,—
I know not how such things can be!—
I breathed my soul back into me.

Ah! Up then from the ground sprang I
And hailed the earth with such a cry
As is not heard save from a man
Who has been dead, and lives again.
About the trees my arms I wound;
Like one gone mad I hugged the ground;
I raised my quivering arms on high;
I laughed and laughed into the sky;
Till at my throat a strangling sob
Caught fiercely, and a great heart-throb
Sent instant tears into my eyes:
O God, I cried, no dark disguise
Can e'er hereafter hide from me
Thy radiant identity!
Thou canst not move across the grass
But my quick eyes will see Thee pass,
Nor speak, however silently,
But my hushed voice will answer Thee.
I know the path that tells Thy way
Through the cool eve of every day;

God, I can push the grass apart
And lay my finger on Thy heart!

The world stands out on either side
No wider than the heart is wide;
Above the world is stretched the sky,—
No higher than the soul is high.
The heart can push the sea and land
Farther away on either hand;
The soul can split the sky in two,
And let the face of God shine through.
But East and West will pinch the heart
That can not keep them pushed apart;
And he whose soul is flat—the sky
Will cave in on him by and by.

AFTERNOON ON A HILL

I will be the gladdest thing
    Under the sun!
I will touch a hundred flowers
    And not pick one.

I will look at cliffs and clouds
    With quiet eyes,
Watch the wind bow down the grass,
    And the grass rise.

And when lights begin to show
    Up from the town,
I will mark which must be mine,
    And then start down!

WITCH-WIFE

She is neither pink nor pale,
   And she never will be all mine;
She learned her hands in a fairy-tale,
   And her mouth on a valentine.

She has more hair than she needs;
   In the sun 'tis a woe to me!
And her voice is a string of coloured beads,
   Or steps leading into the sea.

She loves me all that she can,
   And her ways to my ways resign;
But she was not made for any man,
   And she never will be all mine.

Y

Time does not bring relief; you all have lied
Who told me time would ease me of my pain!
I miss him in the weeping of the rain;
I want him at the shrinking of the tide;
The old snows melt from every mountain-side,
And last year's leaves are smoke in every lane;
But last year's bitter loving must remain
Heaped on my heart, and my old thoughts abide.
There are a hundred places where I fear
To go,—so with his memory they brim.
And entering with relief some quiet place
Where never fell his foot or shone his face
I say, "There is no memory of him here!"
And so stand stricken, so remembering him.

Y

If I should learn, in some quite casual way,
That you were gone, not to return again—
Read from the back-page of a paper, say,
Held by a neighbor in a subway train,
How at the corner of this avenue
And such a street (so are the papers filled)
A hurrying man, who happened to be you,
At noon today had happened to be killed—
I should not cry aloud—I could not cry
Aloud, or wring my hands in such a place—
I should but watch the station lights rush by
With a more careful interest on my face;
Or raise my eyes and read with greater care
Where to store furs and how to treat the hair.

BLUEBEARD

This door you might not open, and you did;
So enter now, and see for what slight thing
You are betrayed. . . . Here is no treasure hid,
No cauldron, no clear crystal mirroring
The sought-for Truth, no heads of women slain
For greed like yours, no writhings of distress;
But only what you see. . . . Look yet again:
An empty room, cobwebbed and comfortless.
Yet this alone out of my life I kept
Unto myself, lest any know me quite;
And you did so profane me when you crept
Unto the threshold of this room tonight
That I must never more behold your face.
This now is yours. I seek another place.

FROM
*A FEW FIGS
FROM THISTLES*
(1920)

FIRST FIG

My candle burns at both ends;
   It will not last the night;
But ah, my foes, and oh, my friends—
   It gives a lovely light!

SECOND FIG

Safe upon the solid rock the ugly houses stand:
Come and see my shining palace built upon the sand!

RECUERDO

We were very tired, we were very merry—
We had gone back and forth all night on the ferry.
It was bare and bright, and smelled like a stable—
But we looked into a fire, we leaned across a table,
We lay on a hill-top underneath the moon;
And the whistles kept blowing, and the dawn came soon.

We were very tired, we were very merry—
We had gone back and forth all night on the ferry;
And you ate an apple, and I ate a pear,
From a dozen of each we had bought somewhere;
And the sky went wan, and the wind came cold,
And the sun rose dripping, a bucketful of gold.

We were very tired, we were very merry,
We had gone back and forth all night on the ferry.
We hailed, "Good morrow, mother!" to a shawl-covered head,
And bought a morning paper, which neither of us read;
And she wept, "God bless you!" for the apples and pears,
And we gave her all our money but our subway fares.

To the Not Impossible Him

How shall I know, unless I go
    To Cairo and Cathay,
Whether or not this blessèd spot
    Is blest in every way?

Now it may be, the flower for me
    Is this beneath my nose;
How shall I tell, unless I smell
    The Carthaginian rose?

The fabric of my faithful love
    No power shall dim or ravel
Whilst I stay here,—but oh, my dear,
    If I should ever travel!

THE UNEXPLORER

There was a road ran past our house
Too lovely to explore.
I asked my mother once—she said
That if you followed where it led
It brought you to the milk-man's door.
(That's why I have not travelled more.)

GROWN-UP

Was it for this I uttered prayers,
And sobbed and cursed and kicked the stairs,
That now, domestic as a plate,
I should retire at half-past eight?

THE PHILOSOPHER

And what are you that, wanting you,
   I should be kept awake
As many nights as there are days
   With weeping for your sake?

And what are you that, missing you,
   As many days as crawl
I should be listening to the wind
   And looking at the wall?

I know a man that's a braver man
   And twenty men as kind,
And what are you, that you should be
   The one man in my mind?

Yet women's ways are witless ways,
   As any sage will tell,—
And what am I, that I should love
   So wisely and so well?

Υ

I think I should have loved you presently,
And given in earnest words I flung in jest;
And lifted honest eyes for you to see,
And caught your hand against my cheek and breast;
And all my pretty follies flung aside
That won you to me, and beneath your gaze,
Naked of reticence and shorn of pride,
Spread like a chart my little wicked ways.
I, that had been to you, had you remained,
But one more waking from a recurrent dream,
Cherish no less the certain stakes I gained,
And walk your memory's halls, austere, supreme,
A ghost in marble of a girl you knew
Who would have loved you in a day or two.

Y

I shall forget you presently, my dear,
So make the most of this, your little day,
Your little month, your little half a year,
Ere I forget, or die, or move away,
And we are done forever; by and by
I shall forget you, as I said, but now,
If you entreat me with your loveliest lie
I will protest you with my favourite vow.
I would indeed that love were longer-lived,
And oaths were not so brittle as they are,
But so it is, and nature has contrived
To struggle on without a break thus far,—
Whether or not we find what we are seeking
Is idle, biologically speaking.

FROM

SECOND APRIL

(1921)

SPRING

To what purpose, April, do you return again?
Beauty is not enough.
You can no longer quiet me with the redness
Of little leaves opening stickily.
I know what I know.
The sun is hot on my neck as I observe
The spikes of the crocus.
The smell of the earth is good.
It is apparent that there is no death.
But what does that signify?
Not only under ground are the brains of men
Eaten by maggots.
Life in itself
Is nothing,
An empty cup, a flight of uncarpeted stairs.
It is not enough that yearly, down this hill,
April
Comes like an idiot, babbling and strewing flowers.

WEEDS

White with daisies and red with sorrel
    And empty, empty under the sky!—
Life is a quest and love a quarrel—
    Here is a place for me to lie.

Daisies spring from damnèd seeds,
    And this red fire that here I see
Is a worthless crop of crimson weeds,
    Cursed by farmers thriftily.

But here, unhated for an hour,
    The sorrel runs in ragged flame,
The daisy stands, a bastard flower,
    Like flowers that bear an honest name.

And here a while, where no wind brings
    The baying of a pack athirst,
May sleep the sleep of blessèd things,
    The blood too bright, the brow accurst.

PASSER MORTUUS EST

Death devours all lovely things:
  Lesbia with her sparrow
Shares the darkness,—presently
  Every bed is narrow.

Unremembered as old rain
  Dries the sheer libation;
And the little petulant hand
  Is an annotation.

After all, my erstwhile dear,
  My no longer cherished,
Need we say it was not love,
  Just because it perished?

ASSAULT

I had forgotten how the frogs must sound
After a year of silence, else I think
I should not so have ventured forth alone
At dusk upon this unfrequented road.

I am waylaid by Beauty. Who will walk
Between me and the crying of the frogs?
Oh, savage Beauty, suffer me to pass,
That am a timid woman, on her way
From one house to another!

TRAVEL

The railroad track is miles away,
 And the day is loud with voices speaking,
Yet there isn't a train goes by all day
 But I hear its whistle shrieking.

All night there isn't a train goes by,
 Though the night is still for sleep and dreaming,
But I see its cinders red on the sky,
 And hear its engine steaming.

My heart is warm with the friends I make,
 And better friends I'll not be knowing;
Yet there isn't a train I wouldn't take,
 No matter where it's going.

ALMS

My heart is what it was before,
 A house where people come and go;
But it is winter with your love,
 The sashes are beset with snow.

I light the lamp and lay the cloth,
 I blow the coals to blaze again;
But it is winter with your love,
 The frost is thick upon the pane.

I know a winter when it comes:
 The leaves are listless on the boughs;
I watched your love a little while,
 And brought my plants into the house.

I water them and turn them south,
 I snap the dead brown from the stem;
But it is winter with your love,
 I only tend and water them.

There was a time I stood and watched
 The small, ill-natured sparrows' fray;
I loved the beggar that I fed,
 I cared for what he had to say,

I stood and watched him out of sight;
 Today I reach around the door

And set a bowl upon the step;
  My heart is what it was before,

But it is winter with your love;
  I scatter crumbs upon the sill,
And close the window,—and the birds
  May take or leave them, as they will.

INLAND

People that build their houses inland,
  People that buy a plot of ground
Shaped like a house, and build a house there,
  Far from the sea-board, far from the sound

Of water sucking the hollow ledges,
  Tons of water striking the shore,—
What do they long for, as I long for
  One salt smell of the sea once more?

People the waves have not awakened,
  Spanking the boats at the harbour's head,
What do they long for, as I long for,—
  Starting up in my inland bed,

Beating the narrow walls, and finding
  Neither a window nor a door,
Screaming to God for death by drowning,—
  One salt taste of the sea once more?

(Vassar College, 1918)

O, loveliest throat of all sweet throats,
Where now no more the music is,
With hands that wrote you little notes
I write you little elegies!

V

Elegy

Let them bury your big eyes
In the secret earth securely,
Your thin fingers, and your fair,
Soft, indefinite-coloured hair,—
All of these in some way, surely,
From the secret earth shall rise;
Not for these I sit and stare,
Broken and bereft completely:
Your young flesh that sat so neatly
On your little bones will sweetly
Blossom in the air.

But your voice . . . never the rushing
Of a river underground,
Not the rising of the wind
In the trees before the rain,
Not the woodcock's watery call,
Not the note the white-throat utters,
Not the feet of children pushing

37

Yellow leaves along the gutters
In the blue and bitter fall,
Shall content my musing mind
For the beauty of that sound
That in no new way at all
Ever will be heard again.

Sweetly through the sappy stalk
Of the vigourous weed,
Holding all it held before,
Cherished by the faithful sun,
On and on eternally
Shall your altered fluid run,
Bud and bloom and go to seed:
But your singing days are done;
But the music of your talk
Never shall the chemistry
Of the secret earth restore.
All your lovely words are spoken.
Once the ivory box is broken,
Beats the golden bird no more.

WILD SWANS

I looked in my heart while the wild swans went over.
And what did I see I had not seen before?
Only a question less or a question more;
Nothing to match the flight of wild birds flying.
Tiresome heart, forever living and dying,
House without air, I leave you and lock your door.
Wild swans, come over the town, come over
The town again, trailing your legs and crying!

FROM

THE HARP-WEAVER

AND OTHER POEMS

(1 9 2 3)

NUIT BLANCHE

I am a shepherd of those sheep
   That climb a wall by night,
One after one, until I sleep,
   Or the black pane goes white.
Because of which I cannot see
   A flock upon a hill,
But doubts come tittering up to me
   That should by day be still.
And childish griefs I have outgrown
   Into my eyes are thrust,
Till my dull tears go dropping down
   Like lead into the dust.

III

Rain comes down
And hushes the town.
And where is the voice that I heard crying?

Snow settles
Over the nettles.
Where is the voice that I heard crying?

Sand at last
On the drifting mast.
And where is the voice that I heard crying?

Earth now
On the busy brow.
And where is the voice that I heard crying?

DEPARTURE

It's little I care what path I take,
And where it leads it's little I care;
But out of this house, lest my heart break,
I must go, and off somewhere.

It's little I know what's in my heart,
What's in my mind it's little I know,
But there's that in me must up and start,
And it's little I care where my feet go.

I wish I could walk for a day and a night,
And find me at dawn in a desolate place
With never the rut of a road in sight,
Nor the roof of a house, nor the eyes of a face.

I wish I could walk till my blood should spout,
And drop me, never to stir again,
On a shore that is wide, for the tide is out,
And the weedy rocks are bare to the rain.

But dump or dock, where the path I take
Brings up, it's little enough I care;
And it's little I'd mind the fuss they'll make,
Huddled dead in a ditch somewhere.

"Is something the matter, dear," she said,
"That you sit at your work so silently?"

"No, mother, no, 'twas a knot in my thread.
There goes the kettle, I'll make the tea."

HUMORESQUE

"Heaven bless the babe!" they said.
"What queer books she must have read!"
(Love, by whom I was beguiled,
Grant I may not bear a child.)

"Little does she guess to-day
What the world may be!" they say.
(Snow, drift deep and cover
Till the spring my murdered lover.)

Never May the Fruit Be Plucked

Never, never may the fruit be plucked from the bough
And gathered into barrels.
He that would eat of love must eat it where it hangs.
Though the branches bend like reeds,
Though the ripe fruit splash in the grass or wrinkle on the
     tree,
He that would eat of love may bear away with him
Only what his belly can hold,
Nothing in the apron,
Nothing in the pockets.
Never, never may the fruit be gathered from the bough
And harvested in barrels.
The winter of love is a cellar of empty bins,
In an orchard soft with rot.

THE CONCERT

No, I will go alone.
I will come back when it's over.
Yes, of course I love you.
No, it will not be long.
Why may you not come with me?—
You are too much my lover.
You would put yourself
Between me and song.

If I go alone,
Quiet and suavely clothed,
My body will die in its chair,
And over my head a flame,
A mind that is twice my own,
Will mark with icy mirth
The wide advance and retreat
Of armies without a country,
Storming a nameless gate,
Hurling terrible javelins down
From the shouting walls of a singing town
Where no women wait!
Armies clean of love and hate,
Marching lines of pitiless sound
Climbing hills to the sun and hurling
Golden spears to the ground!
Up the lines a silver runner
Bearing a banner whereon is scored

The milk and steel of a bloodless wound
Healed at length by the sword!

You and I have nothing to do with music.
We may not make of music a filigree frame,
Within which you and I,
Tenderly glad we came,
Sit smiling, hand in hand.

Come now, be content.
I will come back to you, I swear I will;
And you will know me still.
I shall be only a little taller
Than when I went.

SIEGE

This I do, being mad:
Gather baubles about me,
Sit in a circle of toys, and all the time
Death beating the door in.

White jade and an orange pitcher,
Hindu idol, Chinese god,—
Maybe next year, when I'm richer—
Carved beads and a lotus pod . . .

And all this time
Death beating the door in.

THE CAIRN

When I think of the little children learning
In all the schools of the world,
Learning in Danish, learning in Japanese
That two and two are four, and where the rivers of the world
Rise, and the names of the mountains and the principal cities,
My heart breaks.
Come up, children! Toss your little stones gaily
On the great cairn of Knowledge!
(Where lies what Euclid knew, a little grey stone,
What Plato, what Pascal, what Galileo:
Little grey stones, little grey stones on a cairn.)
Tell me, what is the name of the highest mountain?
Name me a crater of fire! a peak of snow!
Name me the mountains on the moon!
But the name of the mountain that you climb all day,
Ask not your teacher that.

Y

Pity me not because the light of day
At close of day no longer walks the sky;
Pity me not for beauties passed away
From field and thicket as the year goes by;
Pity me not the waning of the moon,
Nor that the ebbing tide goes out to sea,
Nor that a man's desire is hushed so soon,
And you no longer look with love on me.
This have I known always: Love is no more
Than the wide blossom which the wind assails,
Than the great tide that treads the shifting shore,
Strewing fresh wreckage gathered in the gales:
Pity me that the heart is slow to learn
What the swift mind beholds at every turn.

Y

Oh, oh, you will be sorry for that word!
Give back my book and take my kiss instead.
Was it my enemy or my friend I heard,
"What a big book for such a little head!"
Come, I will show you now my newest hat,
And you may watch me purse my mouth and prink!
Oh, I shall love you still, and all of that.
I never again shall tell you what I think.
I shall be sweet and crafty, soft and sly;
You will not catch me reading any more:
I shall be called a wife to pattern by;
And some day when you knock and push the door,
Some sane day, not too bright and not too stormy,
I shall be gone, and you may whistle for me.

Y

I, being born a woman and distressed
By all the needs and notions of my kind,
Am urged by your propinquity to find
Your person fair, and feel a certain zest
To bear your body's weight upon my breast:
So subtly is the fume of life designed,
To clarify the pulse and cloud the mind,
And leave me once again undone, possessed.
Think not for this, however, the poor treason
Of my stout blood against my staggering brain,
I shall remember you with love, or season
My scorn with pity,—let me make it plain:
I find this frenzy insufficient reason
For conversation when we meet again.

Υ

What lips my lips have kissed, and where, and why,
I have forgotten, and what arms have lain
Under my head till morning; but the rain
Is full of ghosts tonight, that tap and sigh
Upon the glass and listen for reply,
And in my heart there sits a quiet pain
For unremembered lads that not again
Will turn to me at midnight with a cry.
Thus in the winter stands the lonely tree,
Nor knows what birds have vanished one by one,
Yet knows its boughs more silent than before:
I cannot say what loves have come and gone,
I only know that summer sang in me
A little while, that in me sings no more.

From Sonnets from an Ungrafted Tree

I

So she came back into his house again
And watched beside his bed until he died,
Loving him not at all. The winter rain
Splashed in the painted butter-tub outside,
Where once her red geraniums had stood,
Where still their rotted stalks were to be seen;
The thin log snapped; and she went out for wood,
Bareheaded, running the few steps between
The house and shed; there, from the sodden eaves
Blown back and forth on ragged ends of twine,
Saw the dejected creeping-jinny vine,
(And one, big-aproned, blithe, with stiff blue sleeves
Rolled to the shoulder that warm day in spring,
Who planted seeds, musing ahead to their far blossoming).

II

The last white sawdust on the floor was grown
Gray as the first, so long had he been ill;
The axe was nodding in the block; fresh-blown
And foreign came the rain across the sill,
But on the roof so steadily it drummed
She could not think a time it might not be—
In hazy summer, when the hot air hummed
With mowing, and locusts rising raspingly,
When that small bird with iridescent wings
And long incredible sudden silver tongue
Had just flashed (and yet maybe not!) among
The dwarf nasturtiums—when no sagging springs
Of shower were in the whole bright sky, somehow
Upon this roof the rain would drum as it was drum-
     ming now.

III

She filled her arms with wood, and set her chin
Forward, to hold the highest stick in place,
No less afraid than she had always been
Of spiders up her arms and on her face,
But too impatient for a careful search
Or a less heavy loading, from the heap
Selecting hastily small sticks of birch,
For their curled bark, that instantly will leap
Into a blaze, nor thinking to return
Some day, distracted, as of old, to find
Smooth, heavy, round, green logs with a wet, gray rind
Only, and knotty chunks that will not burn,
(That day when dust is on the wood-box floor,
And some old catalogue, and a brown, shriveled apple core).

IV

The white bark writhed and sputtered like a fish
Upon the coals, exuding odorous smoke.
She knelt and blew, in a surging desolate wish
For comfort; and the sleeping ashes woke
And scattered to the hearth, but no thin fire
Broke suddenly, the wood was wet with rain.
Then, softly stepping forth from her desire,
(Being mindful of like passion hurled in vain
Upon a similar task, in other days)
She thrust her breath against the stubborn coal,
Bringing to bear upon its hilt the whole
Of her still body . . . there sprang a little blaze . . .
A pack of hounds, the flame swept up the flue!—
And the blue night stood flattened against the window,
        staring through.

A wagon stopped before the house; she heard
The heavy oilskins of the grocer's man
Slapping against his legs. Of a sudden whirred
Her heart like a frightened partridge, and she ran
And slid the bolt, leaving his entrance free;
Then in the cellar way till he was gone
Hid, breathless, praying that he might not see
The chair sway she had laid her hand upon
In passing. Sour and damp from that dark vault
Arose to her the well-remembered chill;
She saw the narrow wooden stairway still
Plunging into the earth, and the thin salt
Crusting the crocks; until she knew him far,
So stood, with listening eyes upon the empty doughnut jar.

VI

Then cautiously she pushed the cellar door
And stepped into the kitchen—saw the track
Of muddy rubber boots across the floor,
The many paper parcels in a stack
Upon the dresser; with accustomed care
Removed the twine and put the wrappings by,
Folded, and the bags flat, that with an air
Of ease had been whipped open skillfully,
To the gape of children. Treacherously dear
And simple was the dull, familiar task.
And so it was she came at length to ask:
How came the soda there? The sugar here?
Then the dream broke. Silent, she brought the mop,
And forced the trade-slip on the nail that held his razor strop.

VIII

She let them leave their jellies at the door
And go away, reluctant, down the walk.
She heard them talking as they passed before
The blind, but could not quite make out their talk
For noise in the room—the sudden heavy fall
And roll of a charred log, and the roused shower
Of snapping sparks; then sharply from the wall
The unforgivable crowing of the hour.
One instant set ajar, her quiet ear
Was stormed and forced by the full rout of day:
The rasp of a saw, the fussy cluck and bray
Of hens, the wheeze of a pump, she needs must hear;
She inescapably must endure to feel
Across her teeth the grinding of a backing wagon wheel.

IX

Not over-kind nor over-quick in study
Nor skilled in sports nor beautiful was he,
Who had come into her life when anybody
Would have been welcome, so in need was she.
They had become acquainted in this way:
He flashed a mirror in her eyes at school;
By which he was distinguished; from that day
They went about together, as a rule.
She told, in secret and with whispering,
How he had flashed a mirror in her eyes;
And as she told, it struck her with surprise
That this was not so wonderful a thing.
But what's the odds?—It's pretty nice to know
You've got a friend to keep you company everywhere you go.

X

She had forgotten how the August night
Was level as a lake beneath the moon,
In which she swam a little, losing sight
Of shore; and how the boy, who was at noon
Simple enough, not different from the rest,
Wore now a pleasant mystery as he went,
Which seemed to her an honest enough test
Whether she loved him, and she was content.
So loud, so loud the million crickets' choir . . .
So sweet the night, so long-drawn-out and late . . .
And if the man were not her spirit's mate,
Why was her body sluggish with desire?
Stark on the open field the moonlight fell,
But the oak tree's shadow was deep and black and secret as a
    well.

It came into her mind, seeing how the snow
Was gone, and the brown grass exposed again,
And clothes-pins, and an apron—long ago,
In some white storm that sifted through the pane
And sent her forth reluctantly at last
To gather in, before the line gave way,
Garments, board-stiff, that galloped on the blast
Clashing like angel armies in a fray,
An apron long ago in such a night
Blown down and buried in the deepening drift,
To lie till April thawed it back to sight,
Forgotten, quaint and novel as a gift—
It struck her, as she pulled and pried and tore,
That here was spring, and the whole year to be lived through
    once more.

Tenderly, in those times, as though she fed
An ailing child—with sturdy propping up
Of its small, feverish body in the bed,
And steadying of its hands about the cup—
She gave her husband of her body's strength,
Thinking of men, what helpless things they were,
Until he turned and fell asleep at length,
And stealthily stirred the night and spoke to her.
Familiar, at such moments, like a friend,
Whistled far off the long, mysterious train,
And she could see in her mind's vision plain
The magic World, where cities stood on end . . .
Remote from where she lay—and yet—between,
Save for something asleep beside her, only the window screen.

XIV

She had a horror he would die at night.
And sometimes when the light began to fade
She could not keep from noticing how white
The birches looked—and then she would be afraid,
Even with a lamp, to go about the house
And lock the windows; and as night wore on
Toward morning, if a dog howled, or a mouse
Squeaked in the floor, long after it was gone
Her flesh would sit awry on her. By day
She would forget somewhat, and it would seem
A silly thing to go with just this dream
And get a neighbor to come at night and stay.
But it would strike her sometimes, making the tea:
*She had kept that kettle boiling all night long, for com-
    pany.*

The doctor asked her what she wanted done
With him, that could not lie there many days.
And she was shocked to see how life goes on
Even after death, in irritating ways;
And mused how if he had not died at all
'Twould have been easier—then there need not be
The stiff disorder of a funeral
Everywhere, and the hideous industry,
And crowds of people calling her by name
And questioning her, she'd never seen before,
But only watching by his bed once more
And sitting silent if a knocking came . . .
She said at length, feeling the doctor's eyes,
"I don't know what you do exactly when a person dies."

XVII

Gazing upon him now, severe and dead,
It seemed a curious thing that she had lain
Beside him many a night in that cold bed,
And that had been which would not be again.
From his desirous body the great heat
Was gone at last, it seemed, and the taut nerves
Loosened forever. Formally the sheet
Set forth for her today those heavy curves
And lengths familiar as the bedroom door.
She was as one who enters, sly, and proud,
To where her husband speaks before a crowd,
And sees a man she never saw before—
The man who eats his victuals at her side,
Small, and absurd, and hers: for once, not hers, unclassified.

FROM
THE BUCK
IN THE SNOW
(1928)

THE HAWKWEED

Between the red-top and the rye,
  Between the buckwheat and the corn,
The ploughman sees with sullen eye
The hawkweed licking at the sky:

   Three level acres all forlorn,
   Unfertile, sour, outrun, outworn,
   Free as the day that they were born.

Southward and northward, west and east,
  The sulphate and the lime are spread;
Harrowed and sweetened, urged, increased,
The furrow sprouts for man and beast:

   While of the hawkweed's radiant head
   No stanchion reeks, no stock is fed.

Triumphant up the taken field
  The tractor and the plough advance;
Blest be the healthy germ concealed
In the rich earth, and blest the yield:

   And blest be Beauty, that enchants
   The frail, the solitary lance.

FOR PAO-CHIN, A BOATMAN ON THE YELLOW SEA

Where is he now, in his soiled shirt reeking of garlic,
Sculling his sampan home, and night approaching fast—
The red sail hanging wrinkled on the bamboo mast;

Where is he now, I shall remember my whole life long
With love and praise, for the sake of a small song
Played on a Chinese flute?
                                            I have been sad;
I have been in cities where the song was all I had,—
A treasure never to be bartered by the hungry days.

Where is he now, for whom I carry in my heart
This love, this praise?

THE BUCK IN THE SNOW

White sky, over the hemlocks bowed with snow,
Saw you not at the beginning of evening the antlered buck and
    his doe
Standing in the apple-orchard? I saw them. I saw them sud-
    denly go,
Tails up, with long leaps lovely and slow,
Over the stone-wall into the wood of hemlocks bowed with
    snow.

Now lies he here, his wild blood scalding the snow.

How strange a thing is death, bringing to his knees, bringing
    to his antlers
The buck in the snow.
How strange a thing,—a mile away by now, it may be,
Under the heavy hemlocks that as the moments pass
Shift their loads a little, letting fall a feather of snow—
Life, looking out attentive from the eyes of the doe.

JUSTICE DENIED IN MASSACHUSETTS*

Let us abandon then our gardens and go home
And sit in the sitting-room.
Shall the larkspur blossom or the corn grow under this cloud?
Sour to the fruitful seed
Is the cold earth under this cloud,
Fostering quack and weed, we have marched upon but cannot
        conquer;
We have bent the blades of our hoes against the stalks of them.

Let us go home, and sit in the sitting-room.
Not in our day
Shall the cloud go over and the sun rise as before,
Beneficent upon us
Out of the glittering bay,
And the warm winds be blown inward from the sea
Moving the blades of corn
With a peaceful sound.
Forlorn, forlorn,
Stands the blue hay-rack by the empty mow.
And the petals drop to the ground,
Leaving the tree unfruited.
The sun that warmed our stooping backs and withered the
        weed uprooted—
We shall not feel it again.
We shall die in darkness, and be buried in the rain.

* This poem relates to the murder trial of Nicola Sacco and Bartolomeo Vanzetti
and their execution on 22 August 1927.

What from the splendid dead
We have inherited—
Furrows sweet to the grain, and the weed subdued—
See now the slug and the mildew plunder.
Evil does overwhelm
The larkspur and the corn;
We have seen them go under.

Let us sit here, sit still,
Here in the sitting-room until we die;
At the step of Death on the walk, rise and go;
Leaving to our children's children this beautiful doorway,
And this elm,
And a blighted earth to till
With a broken hoe.

To Those Without Pity

Cruel of heart, lay down my song.
Your reading eyes have done me wrong.
Not for you was the pen bitten,
And the mind wrung, and the song written.

DIRGE WITHOUT MUSIC

I am not resigned to the shutting away of loving hearts in the
    hard ground.
So it is, and so it will be, for so it has been, time out of mind:
Into the darkness they go, the wise and the lovely. Crowned
With lilies and with laurel they go; but I am not resigned.

Lovers and thinkers, into the earth with you.
Be one with the dull, the indiscriminate dust.
A fragment of what you felt, of what you knew,
A formula, a phrase remains,—but the best is lost.

The answers quick and keen, the honest look, the laughter,
    the love,—
They are gone. They are gone to feed the roses. Elegant and
    curled
Is the blossom. Fragrant is the blossom. I know. But I do not
    approve.
More precious was the light in your eyes than all the roses in
    the world.

Down, down, down into the darkness of the grave
Gently they go, the beautiful, the tender, the kind;
Quietly they go, the intelligent, the witty, the brave.
I know. But I do not approve. And I am not resigned.

MEMORY OF CASSIS

Do you recall how we sat by the smokily-burning
Twisted odourous trunk of the olive-tree,
In the inn on the cliff, and skinned the ripe green figs,
And heard the white sirocco driving in the sea?

The thunder and the smother there where like a ship's prow
The light-house breasted the wave? how wanly through the
    wild spray
Under our peering eyes the eye of the light looked out,
Disheveled, but without dismay?

Do you recall the sweet-alyssum over the ledges
Crawling and the tall heather and the mushrooms under the
    pines,
And the deep white dust of the broad road leading outward
To a world forgotten, between the dusty almonds and the
    dusty vines?

WINTER NIGHT

Pile high the hickory and the light
Log of chestnut struck by the blight.
Welcome-in the winter night.

The day has gone in hewing and felling,
Sawing and drawing wood to the dwelling
For the night of talk and story-telling.

These are the hours that give the edge
To the blunted axe and the bent wedge,
Straighten the saw and lighten the sledge.

Here are question and reply,
And the fire reflected in the thinking eye.
So peace, and let the bob-cat cry.

THE PLUM GATHERER

The angry nettle and the mild
  Grew together under the blue-plum trees.
I could not tell as a child
  Which was my friend of these.

Always the angry nettle in the skirt of his sister
  Caught my wrist that reached over the ground,
Where alike I gathered,—for the one was sweet and the o
    wore a frosty dust—
  The broken plum and the sound.

The plum-trees are barren now and the black knot is u
    them,
  That stood so white in the spring.
I would give, to recall the sweetness and the frost of the lost
    blue plums,
  Anything, anything.
I thrust my arm among the grey ambiguous nettles, and wait.
  But they do not sting.

FROM

FATAL INTERVIEW

(1 9 3 1)

FROM FATAL INTERVIEW

XXIV

Whereas at morning in a jeweled crown
I bit my fingers and was hard to please,
Having shook disaster till the fruit fell down
I feel tonight more happy and at ease:
Feet running in the corridors, men quick-
Buckling their sword-belts bumping down the stair,
Challenge, and rattling bridge-chain, and the click
Of hooves on pavement—this will clear the air.
Private this chamber as it has not been
In many a month of muffled hours; almost,
Lulled by the uproar, I could lie serene
And sleep, until all's won, until all's lost,
And the door's opened and the issue shown,
And I walk forth Hell's mistress . . . or my own.

Love is not all: it is not meat nor drink
Nor slumber nor a roof against the rain;
Nor yet a floating spar to men that sink
And rise and sink and rise and sink again;
Love can not fill the thickened lung with breath,
Nor clean the blood, nor set the fractured bone;
Yet many a man is making friends with death
Even as I speak, for lack of love alone.
It well may be that in a difficult hour,
Pinned down by pain and moaning for release,
Or nagged by want past resolution's power,
I might be driven to sell your love for peace,
Or trade the memory of this night for food.
It well may be. I do not think I would.

Hearing your words, and not a word among them
Tuned to my liking, on a salty day
When inland woods were pushed by winds that flung them
Hissing to leeward like a ton of spray,
I thought how off Matinicus the tide
Came pounding in, came running through the Gut,
While from the Rock the warning whistle cried,
And children whimpered, and the doors blew shut;
There in the autumn when the men go forth,
With slapping skirts the island women stand
In gardens stripped and scattered, peering north,
With dahlia tubers dripping from the hand:
The wind of their endurance, driving south,
Flattened your words against your speaking mouth.

Love me no more, now let the god depart,
If love be grown so bitter to your tongue!
Here is my hand; I bid you from my heart
Fare well, fare very well, be always young.
As for myself, mine was a deeper drouth:
I drank and thirsted still; but I surmise
My kisses now are sand against your mouth,
Teeth in your palm and pennies on your eyes.
Speak but one cruel word, to shame my tears;
Go, but in going, stiffen up my back
To meet the yelping of the mustering years—
Dim, trotting shapes that seldom will attack
Two with a light who match their steps and sing:
To one alone and lost, another thing.

Now by the path I climbed, I journey back.
The oaks have grown; I have been long away.
Taking with me your memory and your lack
I now descend into a milder day;
Stripped of your love, unburdened of my hope,
Descend the path I mounted from the plain;
Yet steeper than I fancied seems the slope
And stonier, now that I go down again.
Warm falls the dusk; the clanking of a bell
Faintly ascends upon this heavier air;
I do recall those grassy pastures well:
In early spring they drove the cattle there.
And close at hand should be a shelter, too,
From which the mountain peaks are not in view.

FROM
WINE FROM
THESE GRAPES
(1 9 3 4)

THE RETURN

Earth does not understand her child,
　Who from the loud gregarious town
Returns, depleted and defiled,
　To the still woods, to fling him down.

Earth can not count the sons she bore:
　The wounded lynx, the wounded man
Come trailing blood unto her door;
　She shelters both as best she can.

But she is early up and out,
　To trim the year or strip its bones;
She has no time to stand about
　Talking of him in undertones

Who has no aim but to forget,
　Be left in peace, be lying thus
For days, for years, for centuries yet,
　Unshaven and anonymous;

Who, marked for failure, dulled by grief,
　Has traded in his wife and friend
For this warm ledge, this alder leaf:
　Comfort that does not comprehend.

THE OAK-LEAVES

Yet in the end, defeated too, worn out and ready to fall,
Hangs from the drowsy tree with cramped and desperate stem
    above the ditch the last leaf of all.

There is something to be learned, I guess, from looking at the
    dead leaves under the living tree;
Something to be set to a lusty tune and learned and sung, it
    well might be;
Something to be learned—though I was ever a ten-o'clock
    scholar at this school—
Even perhaps by me.

But my heart goes out to the oak-leaves that are the last to sigh
"Enough," and loose their hold;
They have boasted to the nudging frost and to the two-and-
    thirty winds that they would never die,
Never even grow old.
(These are those russet leaves that cling
All winter, even into the spring,
To the dormant bough, in the wood knee-deep in snow the
    only coloured thing.)

The Hedge of Hemlocks

Somebody long ago
Set out this hedge of hemlocks; brought from the woods, I'd
    say,
Saplings ten inches tall, curving and delicate, not shaped like
    trees,
And set them out, to shut the marshes from the lawn,
A hedge of ferns.

Four feet apart he set them, far apart, leaving them room to
    grow . . .
Whose crowded lower boughs these fifty years at least
Are spiky stumps outthrust in all directions, dry, dropping
    scaly bark, in the deep shade making a thick
Dust which here and there floats in a short dazzling beam.

Green tops, delicate and curving yet, above this fence of brush,
    like ferns,
You have done well: more than the marshes now is shut away
    from his protected dooryard;
The mountain, too, is shut away; not even the wind
May trespass here to stir the purple phlox in the tall grass.

And yet how easily one afternoon between
Your stems, unheard, snapping no twig, dislodging no shell of
    loosened bark, unseen
Even by the spider through whose finished web he walked, and
    left it as he found it,
A neighbour entered.

CAP D'ANTIBES

The storm is over, and the land has forgotten the storm; the
    trees are still.
Under this sun the rain dries quickly.
Cones from the sea-pines cover the ground again
Where yesterday for my fire I gathered all in sight;
But the leaves are meek. The smell of the small alyssum that
    grows wild here
Is in the air. It is a childish morning.

More sea than land am I; my sulky mind, whipped high by
    tempest in the night, is not so soon appeased.
Into my occupations with dull roar
It washes,
It recedes.
Even as at my side in the calm day the disturbed Mediterra-
    nean
Lurches with heavy swell against the bird-twittering shore.

FROM A TRAIN WINDOW

Precious in the light of the early sun the Housatonic
Between its not unscalable mountains flows.
Precious in the January morning the shabby fur of the cat-tails
    by the stream.
The farmer driving his horse to the feed-store for a sack of
    cracked corn
Is not in haste; there is no whip in the socket.

Pleasant enough, gay even, by no means sad
Is the rickety graveyard on the hill. Those are not cypress trees
Perpendicular among the lurching slabs, but cedars from the
    neighbourhood,
Native to this rocky land, self-sown. Precious
In the early light, reassuring
Is the grave-scarred hillside.
As if after all, the earth might know what it is about.

THE FAWN

There it was I saw what I shall never forget
And never retrieve.
Monstrous and beautiful to human eyes, hard to believe,
He lay, yet there he lay,
Asleep on the moss, his head on his polished cleft small ebony
    hooves,
The child of the doe, the dappled child of the deer.

Surely his mother had never said, "Lie here
Till I return," so spotty and plain to see
On the green moss lay he.
His eyes had opened; he considered me.

I would have given more than I care to say
To thrifty ears, might I have had him for my friend
One moment only of that forest day:

Might I have had the acceptance, not the love
Of those clear eyes;
Might I have been for him the bough above
Or the root beneath his forest bed,
A part of the forest, seen without surprise.

Was it alarm, or was it the wind of my fear lest he depart
That jerked him to his jointy knees,
And sent him crashing off, leaping and stumbling
On his new legs, between the stems of the white trees?

SONNET

Time, that renews the tissues of this frame,
That built the child and hardened the soft bone,
Taught him to wail, to blink, to walk alone,
Stare, question, wonder, give the world a name,
Forget the watery darkness whence he came,
Attends no less the boy to manhood grown,
Brings him new raiment, strips him of his own:
All skins are shed at length, remorse, even shame.
Such hope is mine, if this indeed be true,
I dread no more the first white in my hair,
Or even age itself, the easy shoe,
The cane, the wrinkled hands, the special chair:
Time, doing this to me, may alter too
My anguish, into something I can bear.

DESOLATION DREAMED OF

Desolation dreamed of, though not accomplished,
Set my heart to rocking like a boat in a swell.
To every face I met, I said farewell.

Green rollers breaking white along a clean beach . . . when shall I
*   reach that island?*
Gladly, O painted nails and shaven arm-pits, would I see less of you!
Gladly, gladly would I be far from you for a long time, O noise and
*   stench of man!*

I said farewell. Nevertheless,
Whom have I quitted?—which of my possessions do I propose
    to leave?
Not one. This feigning to be asleep when wide awake is all the
    loneliness
I shall ever achieve.

ON THE WIDE HEATH

On the wide heath at evening overtaken,
    When the fast-reddening sun
Drops, and against the sky the looming bracken
    Waves, and the day is done,

Though no unfriendly nostril snuffs his bone,
    Though English wolves be dead,
The fox abroad on errands of his own,
    The adder gone to bed,

The weary traveler from his aching hip
    Lengthens his long stride;
Though Home be but a humming on his lip,
    No happiness, no pride,

He does not drop him under the yellow whin
    To sleep the darkness through;
Home to the yellow light that shines within
    The kitchen of a loud shrew,

Home over stones and sand, through stagnant water
    He goes, mile after mile
Home to a wordless poaching son and a daughter
    With a disdainful smile,

Home to the worn reproach, the disagreeing,
    The shelter, the stale air; content to be

Pecked at, confined, encroached upon,—it being
   Too lonely, to be free.

CONSCIENTIOUS OBJECTOR

I shall die, but that is all that I shall do for Death.

I hear him leading his horse out of the stall; I hear the clatter
    on the barn-floor.
He is in haste; he has business in Cuba, business in the Bal-
    kans, many calls to make this morning.
But I will not hold the bridle while he cinches the girth.
And he may mount by himself: I will not give him a leg up.

Though he flick my shoulders with his whip, I will not tell
    him which way the fox ran.
With his hoof on my breast, I will not tell him where the
    black boy hides in the swamp.
I shall die, but that is all that I shall do for Death; I am not
    on his pay-roll.

I will not tell him the whereabouts of my friends nor of my
    enemies either.
Though he promise me much, I will not map him the route to
    any man's door.

Am I a spy in the land of the living, that I should deliver men
    to Death?
Brother, the password and the plans of our city are safe with
    me; never through me
Shall you be overcome.

ABOVE THESE CARES

Above these cares my spirit in calm abiding
Floats like a swimmer at sunrise, facing the pale sky;
Peaceful, heaved by the light infrequent lurch of the heavy
  wave serenely sliding
Under his weightless body, aware of the wide morning, aware
  of the gull on the red buoy bedaubed with guano, aware
  of his sharp cry;
Idly athirst for the sea, as who should say:
In a moment I will roll upon my mouth and drink it dry.

Painfully, under the pressure that obtains
At the sea's bottom, crushing my lungs and my brains
(For the body makes shift to breathe and after a fashion flourish
Ten fathoms deep in care,
Ten fathoms down in an element denser than air
Wherein the soul must perish)
I trap and harvest, stilling my stomach's needs;
I crawl forever, hoping never to see
Above my head the limbs of my spirit no longer free
Kicking in frenzy, a swimmer enmeshed in weeds.

From Epitaph for the Race of Man

VIII

Observe how Miyanoshita cracked in two
And slid into the valley; he that stood
Grinning with terror in the bamboo wood
Saw the earth heave and thrust its bowels through
The hill, and his own kitchen slide from view,
Spilling the warm bowl of his humble food
Into the lap of horror; mark how lewd
This cluttered gulf,—'twas here his paddy grew.
Dread and dismay have not encompassed him;
The calm sun sets; unhurried and aloof
Into the riven village falls the rain;
Days pass; the ashes cool; he builds again
His paper house upon oblivion's brim,
And plants the purple iris in its roof.

IX

He woke in terror to a sky more bright
Than middle day; he heard the sick earth groan,
And ran to see the lazy-smoking cone
Of the fire-mountain, friendly to his sight
As his wife's hand, gone strange and full of fright;
Over his fleeing shoulder it was shown
Rolling its pitchy lake of scalding stone
Upon his house that had no feet for flight.
Where did he weep? Where did he sit him down
And sorrow, with his head between his knees?
Where said the Race of Man, "Here let me drown"?
"Here let me die of hunger"?—"let me freeze"?
By nightfall he has built another town:
This boiling pot, this clearing in the trees.

X

The broken dike, the levee washed away,
The good fields flooded and the cattle drowned,
Estranged and treacherous all the faithful ground,
And nothing left but floating disarray
Of tree and home uprooted,—was this the day
Man dropped upon his shadow without a sound
And died, having laboured well and having found
His burden heavier than a quilt of clay?
No, no. I saw him when the sun had set
In water, leaning on his single oar
Above his garden faintly glimmering yet . . .
There bulked the plough, here washed the updrifted
    weeds . . .
And scull across his roof and make for shore,
With twisted face and pocket full of seeds.

Now forth to meadow as the farmer goes
With shining buckets to the milking-ground,
He meets the black ant hurrying from his mound
To milk the aphis pastured on the rose;
But no good-morrow, as you might suppose,
No nod of greeting, no perfunctory sound
Passes between them; no occasion's found
For gossip as to how the fodder grows.
In chilly autumn on the hardening road
They meet again, driving their flocks to stall,
Two herdsmen, each with winter for a goad;
They meet and pass, and never a word at all
Gives one to t'other. On the quaint abode
Of each, the evening and the first snow fall.

From
Huntsman,
What Quarry?
(1939)

THE SNOW STORM

No hawk hangs over in this air:
The urgent snow is everywhere.
The wing adroiter than a sail
Must lean away from such a gale,
Abandoning its straight intent,
Or else expose tough ligament
And tender flesh to what before
Meant dampened feathers, nothing more.

Forceless upon our backs there fall
Infrequent flakes hexagonal,
Devised in many a curious style
To charm our safety for a while,
Where close to earth like mice we go
Under the horizontal snow.

Not So Far as the Forest

I

That chill is in the air
Which the wise know well, and even have learned to bear.
This joy, I know,
Will soon be under snow.

The sun sets in a cloud
And is not seen.
Beauty, that spoke aloud,
Addresses now only the remembering ear.
The heart begins here
To feed on what has been.

Night falls fast.
Today is in the past.

Blown from the dark hill hither to my door
Three flakes, then four
Arrive, then many more.

II

Branch by branch
This tree has died. Green only
Is one last bough, moving its leaves in the sun.

What evil ate its root, what blight,
What ugly thing,
Let the mole say, the bird sing;
Or the white worm behind the shedding bark
Tick in the dark.

You and I have only one thing to do:
Saw the trunk through.

III

Distressèd mind, forbear
To tease the hooded Why;
That shape will not reply.

From the warm chair
To the wind's welter
Flee, if storm's your shelter.

But no, you needs must part,
Fling him his release—
On whose ungenerous heart
Alone you are at peace.

IV

Not dead of wounds, not borne
Home to the village on a litter of branches, torn
By splendid claws and the talk all night of the villagers,
But stung to death by gnats
Lies Love.

What swamp I sweated through for all these years
Is at length plain to me.

V

Poor passionate thing,
Even with this clipped wing how well you flew!—though not
    so far as the forest.

Unwounded and unspent, serene but for the eye's bright
    trouble,
Was it the lurching flight, the unequal wind under the lopped
    feathers that brought you down,
To sit in folded colours on the level empty field,
Visible as a ship, paling the yellow stubble?

Rebellious bird, warm body foreign and bright,
Has no one told you?—Hopeless is your flight
Towards the high branches. Here is your home,
Between the barnyard strewn with grain and the forest tree.
Though Time refeather the wing,
Ankle slip the ring,
The once-confined thing
Is never again free.

RENDEZVOUS

Not for these lovely blooms that prank your chambers did I
    come. Indeed,
I could have loved you better in the dark;
That is to say, in rooms less bright with roses, rooms more
    casual, less aware
Of History in the wings about to enter with benevolent air
On ponderous tiptoe, at the cue "Proceed."
Not that I like the ash-trays over-crowded and the place in a
    mess,
Or the monastic cubicle too unctuously austere and stark,
But partly that these formal garlands for our Eighth Street
    Aphrodite are a bit too Greek,
And partly that to make the poor walls rich with our unaided
    loveliness
Would have been more *chic*.

Yet here I am, having told you of my quarrel with the
    taxi-driver over a line of Milton, and you laugh; and you
    are you, none other.
Your laughter pelts my skin with small delicious blows.
But I am perverse: I wish you had not scrubbed—with pum-
    ice, I suppose—
The tobacco stains from your beautiful fingers. And I wish I
    did not feel like your mother.

Modern Declaration

I, having loved ever since I was a child a few things, never
    having wavered
In these affections; never through shyness in the houses of the
    rich or in the presence of clergymen having denied these
    loves;
Never when worked upon by cynics like chiropractors having
    grunted or clicked a vertebra to the discredit of these
    loves;
Never when anxious to land a job having diminished them by
    a conniving smile; or when befuddled by drink
Jeered at them through heartache or lazily fondled the fingers
    of their alert enemies; declare

That I shall love you always.
No matter what party is in power;
No matter what temporarily expedient combination of allied
    interests wins the war;
Shall love you always.

THE FITTING

The fitter said, *Madame, vous avez maigri,"*
And pinched together a handful of skirt at my hip.
"Tant mieux," I said, and looked away slowly, and took my
    under-lip
Softly between my teeth.

               Rip—rip!
Out came the seam, and was pinned together in another
    place.
She knelt before me, a hardworking woman with a familiar
    and unknown face,
Dressed in linty black, very tight in the arm's-eye and smell-
    ing of sweat.
She rose, lifting my arm, and set her cold shears against
    me,—snip-snip;
Her knuckles gouged my breast. My drooped eyes lifted to
    my guarded eyes in the glass, and glanced away as from
    someone they had never met.

"Ah, que madame a maigri!" cried the *vendeuse,* coming in with
    dresses over her arm.
"C'est la chaleur," I said, looking out into the sunny tops of
    the horse-chestnuts—and indeed it was very warm.

I stood for a long time so, looking out into the afternoon,
    thinking of the evening and you. . . .

While they murmured busily in the distance, turning me, touching my secret body, doing what they were paid to do.

"FONTAINE, JE NE BOIRAI PAS DE TON EAU!"

I know I might have lived in such a way
As to have suffered only pain:
Loving not man nor dog;
Not money, even; feeling
Toothache perhaps, but never more than an hour away
From skill and novocaine;
Making no contacts, dealing with life through agents, drink-
    ing one cocktail, betting two dollars, wearing raincoats
    in the rain;
Betrayed at length by no one but the fog
Whispering to the wing of the plane.

"Fountain," I have cried to that unbubbling well, "I will not
    drink of thy water!" Yet I thirst
For a mouthful of—not to swallow, only to rinse my mouth
    in—peace. And while the eyes of the past condemn,
The eyes of the present narrow into assignation. And . . .
    worst . . .
The young are so old, they are born with their fingers crossed;
    I shall get no help from them.

Intention to Escape from Him

I think I will learn some beautiful language, useless for com-
    mercial
Purposes, work hard at that.
I think I will learn the Latin name of every songbird, not only
    in America but wherever they sing.
(Shun meditation, though; invite the controversial:
Is the world flat? Do bats eat cats?) By digging hard I might
    deflect that river, my mind, that uncontrollable thing,
Turgid and yellow, strong to overflow its banks in spring,
    carrying away bridges;
A bed of pebbles now, through which there trickles one clear
    narrow stream, following a course henceforth nefast—

Dig, dig; and if I come to ledges, blast.

THE TRUE ENCOUNTER

"Wolf!" cried my cunning heart
 At every sheep it spied,
 And roused the countryside.

"Wolf! Wolf!"—and up would start
 Good neighbours, bringing spade
 And pitchfork to my aid.

At length my cry was known:
 Therein lay my release.
I met the wolf alone
 And was devoured in peace.

TWO VOICES

First Voice

Let us be circumspect, surrounded as we are
By every foe but one, and he from the woods watching,
Let us be courteous, since we cannot be wise, guilty of no
    neglect, pallid with seemly terror, yet regarding
    with indulgent eyes
Violence, and compromise.

Second Voice

We shall learn nothing; or we shall learn it too late. Why
    should we wait
For Death, who knows the road so well? Need we sit
    hatching—
Such quiet fowl as we, meek to the touch,—a clutch of
    adder's eggs? Let us not turn them; let us not keep
    them warm; let us leave our nests and flock and tell
All that we know, all that we can piece together, of a time
    when all went, or seemed to go, well.

THE PRINCESS RECALLS HER ONE ADVENTURE

Hard is my pillow
Of down from the duck's breast,
Harsh the linen cover;
I cannot rest.

Fall down, my tears,
Upon the fine hem,
Upon the lonely letters
Of my long name;
Drown the sigh of them.

We stood by the lake
And we neither kissed nor spoke;
We heard how the small waves
Lurched and broke,
And chuckled in the rock.

We spoke and turned away.
We never kissed at all.
Fall down, my tears.
I wish that you might fall
On the road by the lake,
Where my cob went lame,
And I stood with the groom
Till the carriage came.

Y

I too beneath your moon, almighty Sex,
Go forth at nightfall crying like a cat,
Leaving the lofty tower I laboured at
For birds to foul and boys and girls to vex
With tittering chalk; and you, and the long necks
Of neighbours sitting where their mothers sat
Are well aware of shadowy this and that
In me, that's neither noble nor complex.
Such as I am, however, I have brought
To what it is, this tower; it is my own;
Though it was reared To Beauty, it was wrought
From what I had to build with: honest bone
Is there, and anguish; pride; and burning thought;
And lust is there, and nights not spent alone.

FROM

MINE THE HARVEST

(1954)

RAGGED ISLAND

There, there where those black spruces crowd
To the edge of the precipitous cliff,
Above your boat, under the eastern wall of the island;
And no wave breaks; as if
All had been done, and long ago, that needed
Doing; and the cold tide, unimpeded
By shoal or shelving ledge, moves up and down,
Instead of in and out;
And there is no driftwood there, because there is no beach;
Clean cliff going down as deep as clear water can reach;

No driftwood, such as abounds on the roaring shingle,
To be hefted home, for fires in the kitchen stove;
Barrels, banged ashore about the boiling outer harbour;
Lobster-buoys, on the eel-grass of the sheltered cove:

There, thought unbraids itself, and the mind becomes single.
There you row with tranquil oars, and the ocean
Shows no scar from the cutting of your placid keel;
Care becomes senseless there; pride and promotion
Remote; you only look; you scarcely feel.

Even adventure, with its vital uses,
Is aimless ardour now; and thrift is waste.

Oh, to be there, under the silent spruces,
Where the wide, quiet evening darkens without haste
Over a sea with death acquainted, yet forever chaste.

Y

This
Is mine, and I can hold it;
Lying here
In the hour before dawn, knowing that the cruel June
Frost has made the green lawn
White and brittle, smelling that the night was very cold,
Wondering if the lush, well-loved, well-tended,
Hoed and rowed and watched with pride
And with anxiety
So long,—oh, cruel, cruel,
Unseasonable June—
Whether all that green will be black long before noon—

This
I know: that what I hear
Is a thrush; and very near,
Almost on the sill of my open window, close to my ear.
I was startled, but I made no motion, I knew
What I had to do—stop breathing, not be
Here at all, and I have accomplished this. He has not yet
    known
Anything about me; he is singing very loud
And with leisure: he is all alone.

Oh, beautiful, oh, beautiful,
Oh, the most beautiful that I ever have heard,
Anywhere, including the nightingale.
It is not so much the tune

Although the tune is lovely, going suddenly higher
Than you expect, and neat, and, something like the nightin-
	gale dropping
And throbbing very low.
It is not so much the notes, it is the quality of the voice,
Something to do perhaps with over-tone
And under-tone, and implication
Felt, but not quite heard—

Oh, this is much to ask
Of two delicate ear-drums and of some other perception
Which I do not understand, a little oversensitive
Perhaps to certain sounds.
All my senses
Have broken their dikes and flooded into one, the sense of
	hearing.

I have no choice,
I think, if I wish to continue to live: I am beginning to shiver
Already: I may be shattered
Like a vessel too thin
For certain vibrations.
Go away now, I think; go down to the damp hemlocks near
	the brook in the hollow,
Where I cannot quite follow
Your deepest notes, through the dissipating air.
But return soon.

Not so soon, though,
Quite, perhaps,
As tomorrow.

Υ

Few come this way; not that the darkness
Deters them, but they come
Reluctant here who fear to find,
Thickening the darkness, what they left behind
Sucking its cheeks before the fire at home,
The palsied Indecision from whose dancing head
Precipitately they fled, only to come again
Upon him here,
Clutching at the wrist of Venture with a cold
Hand, aiming to fall in with him, companion
Of the new as of the old.

New England Spring, 1942

The rush of rain against the glass
Is louder than my noisy mind
Crying, "Alas!"

The rain shouts: "Hear me, how I melt the ice that clamps the
     bent and frozen grass!
Winter cannot come twice
Even this year!
I break it up; I make it water the roots of spring!
I am the harsh beginning, poured in torrents down the hills,
And dripping from the trees and soaking, later, and when the
     wind is still,
Into the roots of flowers, which your eyes, incredulous, soon
     will suddenly find!
Comfort is almost here."

The sap goes up the maple; it drips fast
From the tapped maple into the tin pail
Through tubes of hollow elder; the pails brim;
Birds with scarlet throats and yellow bellies sip from the pail's
     rim.
Snow falls thick; it is sifted
Through cracks about windows and under doors;
It is drifted through hedges into country roads. It cannot last.
Winter is past.
It is hurling back at us boasts of no avail.

But Spring is wise. Pale and with gentle eyes, one day some-
    what she advances;
The next, with a flurry of snow into flake-filled skies retreats
    before the heat in our eyes, and the thing designed
By the sick and longing mind in its lonely fancies—
The sally which would force her and take her.
And Spring is kind.
Should she come running headlong in a wind-whipped acre
Of daffodil skirts down the mountain into this dark valley we
    would go blind.

Here in a Rocky Cup

Here in a rocky cup of earth
The simple acorn brought to birth
What has in ages grown to be
A very oak, a mighty tree.
The granite of the rock is split
And crumbled by the girth of it.

Incautious was the rock to feed
The acorn's mouth; unwise indeed
Am I, upon whose stony heart
Fell softly down, sits quietly,
The seed of love's imperial tree
That soon may force my breast apart.

"I fear you not. I have no doubt
My meagre soil shall starve you out!"

Unless indeed you prove to be
The kernel of a kingly tree;
Which if you be I am content
To go the way the granite went,
And be myself no more at all,
So you but prosper and grow tall.

Υ

How innocent we lie among
The righteous!—Lord, how sweet we smell,
Doing this wicked thing, this love,
Bought up by bishops!—doing well,
With all our leisure, all our pride,
What's illy done and done in haste
By licensed folk on every side,
Spitting out fruit before they taste.

(That stalk must thrust a clubby bud;
Push an abortive flower to birth.)

Under the moon and the lit scud
Of the clouds, the cool conniving earth
Pillows my head, where your head lies;

Weep, if you must, into my hair
Tomorrow's trouble: the cold eyes
That know you gone and wonder where.
But tell the bishops with their sons,
Shout to the City Hall how we
Under a thick barrage of guns
Filched their divine commodity.

ARMENONVILLE

By the lake at Armenonville in the Bois de Boulogne
Small begonias had been set in the embankment, both pink
    and red;
With polished leaf and brittle, juicy stem;
They covered the embankment; there were wagon-loads of
    them,
Charming and neat, gay colours in the warm shade.

We had preferred a table near the lake, half out of view,
Well out of hearing, for a voice not raised above
A low, impassioned question and its low reply.
We both leaned forward with our elbows on the table, and you
Watched my mouth while I answered, and it made me shy.
I looked about, but the waiters knew we were in love,
And matter-of-factly left us blissfully alone.

There swam across the lake, as I looked aside, avoiding
Your eyes for a moment, there swam from under the pink and
    red begonias
A small creature; I thought it was a water-rat; it swam very
    well,
In complete silence, and making no ripples at all
Hardly; and when suddenly I turned again to you,
Aware that you were speaking, and perhaps had been speaking
    for some time,
I was aghast at my absence, for truly I did not know
Whether you had been asking or telling.

IV

Heavily on the faithful bulk of Kurvenal,
My servant for a long time, leaning,
With footsteps less from weakness than for pleasure in the
    green grass, lagging, I came here,
Out of the house, to lie, propped up on pillows, under this fine
    tree—
Oak older than I, but still, not being ill, growing,
Granted to feel, I think, barring lightning, year after year,—
    and barring the axe—
For a long time yet, the green sap flowing.

Y

When the tree-sparrows with no sound through the pearl-pale
    air
Of dawn, down the apple-branches, stair by stair,
With utmost, unforgettable, elegance and grace
Descended to the bare ground (never bare
Of small strewn seeds
For forced-down flyers at this treacherous time of year),
And richly and sweetly twittered there,
I pressed my forehead to the window, butting the cold glass
Till I feared it might break, disturbing the sparrows, so let the
    moment pass
When I had hoped to recapture the rapture of my dark dream;
I had heard as I awoke my own voice thinly scream,
"Where? in what street? (I knew the city) did they attack
You, bound for home?"
You were, of course, not there.
And I of course wept, remembering where I last had met you,
Yet clawed with desperate nails at the sliding dream, scream-
    ing not to lose, since I cannot forget you.

I felt the hot tears come;
Streaming with useless tears, which make the ears roar and the
    eyelids swell,
My blind face sought the window-sill
To cry on—frozen mourning melted by sly sleep,
Slapping hard-bought repose with quick successive blows until
    it whimper and outright weep.

The tide pulls twice a day,
The sunlit and the moonlit tides
Drag the rough ledge away
And bring back seaweed, little else besides.
Oh, do not weep these tears salter than the flung spray!—
Weepers are the sea's brides . . .
I mean this the drowning way.

CAVE CANEM

Importuned through the mails, accosted over the telephone,
    overtaken by running footsteps, caught by the sleeve, the
    servant of strangers,
While amidst the haste and confusion lover and friend quietly
    step into the unreachable past,
I throw bright time to chickens in an untidy yard.

Through foul timidity, through a gross indisposition to excite
    the ill-will of even the most negligible,
Disliking voices raised in anger, faces with no love in them,
I avoid the looming visitor,
Flee him adroitly around corners,
Hating him, wishing him well;

Lest if he confront me I be forced to say what is in no wise
    true:
That he is welcome; that I am unoccupied;
And forced to sit while the potted roses wilt in the crate or the
    sonnet cools
Bending a respectful nose above such dried philosophies
As have hung in wreaths from the rafters of my house since I
    was a child.

Some trace of kindliness in this, no doubt,
There may be.
But not enough to keep a bird alive.

There is a flaw amounting to a fissure
In such behaviour.

AN ANCIENT GESTURE

I thought, as I wiped my eyes on the corner of my apron:
Penelope did this too.
And more than once: you can't keep weaving all day
And undoing it all through the night;
Your arms get tired, and the back of your neck gets tight;
And along towards morning, when you think it will never be
     light,
And your husband has been gone, and you don't know where,
     for years,
Suddenly you burst into tears;
There is simply nothing else to do.

And I thought, as I wiped my eyes on the corner of my apron:
This is an ancient gesture, authentic, antique,
In the very best tradition, classic, Greek;
Ulysses did this too.
But only as a gesture,—a gesture which implied
To the assembled throng that he was much too moved to
     speak.
He learned it from Penelope . . .
Penelope, who really cried.

Υ

Establishment is shocked. Stir no adventure
Upon this splitted granite.

I will no longer connive
At my own destruction:—I will not again climb,
Breaking my finger nails, out of reach of the reaching wave,
To save
What I hope will still be me
When I have slid on slime and clutched at slippery rock-weed,
        and had my face towed under
In scrubbing pebbles, under the weight of the wave and its
        thunder.
I decline to scratch at this cliff. *If* is not a word.
I will connive no more
With that which hopes and plans that I shall not survive:
Let the tide keep its distance;
Or advance, and be split for a moment by a thing very small
        but all resistance;
Then do its own chore.

SOME THINGS ARE DARK

Some things are dark—or think they are.
But, in comparison to me,
All things are light enough to see
In any place, at any hour.

For I am Nightmare: where I fly,
Terror and rain stand in the sky
So thick, you could not tell them from
That blackness out of which you come.

So much for "where I fly": but when
I strike, and clutch in claw the brain—
Erebus, to such brain, will seem
The thin blue dusk of pleasant dream.

MEN WORKING

Charming, the movement of girls about a May-pole in May,
Weaving the coloured ribbons in and out,
Charming; youth is charming, youth is fair.

But beautiful the movement of men striking pikes
Into the end of a black pole, and slowly
Raising it out of the damp grass and up into the air.
The clean strike of the pike into the pole: beautiful.

Joe is the boss; but Ed or Bill will say,
"No, Joe; we can't get it that way—
We've got to take it from here. Are you okay
On your side, Joe?" "Yes," says the boss. "Okay."

The clean strike of the pike into the pole—*"That's it!"*
"Ground your pikes!"

The grounded pikes about the rising black pole, beautiful.
"Ed, you'd better get under here with me!" "I'm
Under!"
"That's it!"
"Ground your pikes!"

Joe says, "Now, boys, don't heave
Too hard—we've got her—but you, Ed, you and Mike,
You'll have to hold her from underneath while Bill
Shifts his pike—she wants to fall downhill;
We've got her all right, but we've got her on a slight

Slant."
"*That's it!*"—"Mike,
About six feet lower this time."
"*That's it!*"

"*Ground your pikes!*"

One by one the pikes are moved about the pole, more beautiful
Than coloured ribbons weaving.

The clean strike of the pike into the pole; each man
Depending on the skill
And the balance, both of body and of mind,
Of each of the others: in the back of each man's mind
The respect for the pole: it is forty feet high, and weighs
Two thousand pounds.

In the front of each man's mind: "She's going to go
Exactly where we want her to go: this pole
Is going to go into that seven-foot hole we dug
For her
To stand in."

This was in the deepening dusk of a July night.
They were putting in the poles: bringing the electric light.

NOT FOR A NATION

Not for a nation:
Not the dividing, the estranging, thing
For;
Nor, in a world so small, the insulation
Of dream from dream—where dreams are links in the chain
Of a common hope; that man may yet regain
His dignity on earth—where before all
Eyes: small eyes of elephant and shark; still
Eyes of lizard grey in the sub-tropic noon,
Blowing his throat out into a scarlet, edged-with-cream in-
    credible balloon
Suddenly, and suddenly dancing, hoisting and lowering his
    body on his short legs on the hot stone window-sill;
And the eyes of the upturned, grooved and dusty, rounded,
    dull cut-worm
Staring upward at the spade,—
These, all these, and more, from the corner of the eye see
    man, infirm,
Tottering like a tree about to fall,—
Who yet had such high dreams—who not for this was made
    (or so said he),—nor did design to die at all.

Not for a nation,
Not the dividing, the estranging thing
For;
Nor, on a world so small, the insulation
Of dream from dream,
In what might be today, had we been better welders, a new

chain for pulling down old buildings, uprooting the
    wrong trees; these
Not for;
Not for my country right or wrong;
Not for the drum or the bugle; not for the song
Which pipes me away from my home against my will along
    with the other children
To where I would not go
And makes me say what I promised never to say, and do the
    thing I am through with—
Into the Piper's Hill;
Not for the flag
Of any land because myself was born there
Will I give up my life.
But I will love that land where man is free,
And that will I defend.
"To the end?" you ask, "To the end?"—Naturally, to the
    end.

What is it to the world, or to me,
That I beneath an elm, not beneath a tamarisk-tree
First filled my lungs, and clenched my tiny hands already
    spurred and nailed
Against the world, and wailed
In anger and frustration that all my tricks had failed and I
    been torn
Out of the cave where I was hiding, to suffer in the world as
    I have done and I still do—
Never again—oh, no, no more on earth—ever again to find
    abiding-place.
Birth—awful birth . . .

Whatever the country, whatever the colour and race.

The colour and the traits of each,
The shaping of his speech,—
These can the elm, given a long time, alter; these,
Too, the tamarisk.
But if he starve, but if he freeze—
Early, in his own tongue, he knows;
And though with arms or bows or a dipped thorn
Blown through a tube, he fights—the brisk
Rattle of shot he is not slow to tell
From the sound of ripe seed bursting from a poddy shell;
And he whom, all his life, life has abused
Yet knows if he be justly or unjustly used.

I know these elms, this beautiful doorway: here
I am at home, if anywhere.
A natural fondness, an affection which need never be said,
Rises from the wooden sidewalks warm as the smell of new-
        baked bread
From a neighbour's kitchen. It is dusk. The sun goes down.
Sparsely strung along the street the thrifty lights appear.
It is pleasant. It is good.
I am very well-known here; here I am understood.
I can walk along the street, or turn into a path unlighted,
        without fear
Of poisonous snakes, or of any face in town.
Tall elms, my roots go down
As deep as yours into this soil, yes, quite as deep.
And I hear the rocking of my cradle. And I must not sleep.

Not for a nation; not for a little town,
Where, when the sun goes down, you may sit without fear
On the front porch, just out of reach of the arc-light,
    rocking,
With supper ready, wearing a pale new dress, and your baby
    near
In its crib, and your husband due to be home by the next
    trolley that you hear bumping into Elm Street—no:
But for a dream that was dreamt an elm-tree's life ago—
And longer, yes, much longer, and what I mean you know.

For the dream, for the plan, for the freedom of man as it was
    meant
To be;
Not for the structure set up so lustily, by rule of thumb
And over-night, bound to become
Loose, lop-sided, out of plumb,
But for the dream, for the plan, for the freedom of man as it
    was meant
To be
By men with more vision, more wisdom, more purpose,
    more brains
Than we,
(Possibly, possibly)
Men with more courage, men more unselfish, more intent
Than we, upon their dreams, upon their dream of
    Freedom,—Freedom not alone
For oneself, but for all, wherever the word is known,
In whatever tongue, or the longing in whatever spirit—
Men with more honour. (That remains
To be seen! That we shall see!)

Possibly. Possibly.

And if still these truths be held to be
Self-evident.

Υ

It is the fashion now to wave aside
As tedious, obvious, vacuous, trivial, trite,
All things which do not tickle, tease, excite
To some subversion, or in verbiage hide
Intent, or mock, or with hot sauce provide
A dish to prick the thickened appetite;
Straightforwardness is wrong, evasion right;
It is correct, *de rigueur,* to deride.
What fumy wits these modern wags expose,
For all their versatility: Voltaire,
Who wore to bed a night-cap, and would close,
In fear of drafts, all windows, could declare
In antique stuffiness, a phrase that blows
Still through men's smoky minds, and clears the air.

Υ

I will put Chaos into fourteen lines
And keep him there; and let him thence escape
If he be lucky; let him twist, and ape
Flood, fire, and demon—his adroit designs
Will strain to nothing in the strict confines
Of this sweet Order, where, in pious rape,
I hold his essence and amorphous shape,
Till he with Order mingles and combines.
Past are the hours, the years, of our duress,
His arrogance, our awful servitude:
I have him. He is nothing more nor less
Than something simple not yet understood;
I shall not even force him to confess;
Or answer. I will only make him good.

Now sits the autumn cricket in the grass,
And on the gravel crawls the chilly bee;
Near to its close and none too soon for me
Draws the dull year, in which has come to pass
The changing of the happy child I was
Into this quiet creature people see
Stitching a seam with careful industry
To deaden you, who died on Michaelmas.
Ages ago the purple aconite
Laid its dark hoods about it on the ground,
And roses budded small and were content;
Swallows are south long since and out of sight;
With you the phlox and asters also went;
Nor can my laughter anywhere be found.

Υ

What rider spurs him from the darkening east
As from a forest, and with rapid pound
Of hooves, now light, now louder on hard ground,
Approaches, and rides past with speed increased,
Dark spots and flecks of foam upon his beast?
What shouts he from the saddle, turning 'round,
As he rides on?—"Greetings!"—I made the sound;
"Greetings from Nineveh!"—it seemed, at least.
Did someone catch the object that he flung?
He held some object on his saddle-bow,
And flung it towards us as he passed; among
The children then it fell most likely; no,
'Tis here: a little bell without a tongue.
Listen; it has a faint voice even so.

INDEX OF FIRST LINES

How innocent we lie among   136

How shall I know, unless I go   21

I am a shepherd of those sheep   43

I am not resigned to the shutting away of loving hearts in the
hard ground   79

I, being born a woman and distressed   55

I had forgotten how the frogs must sound   32

I, having loved ever since I was a child a few things, never having
wavered   118

I know I might have lived in such a way   121

I looked in my heart while the wild swans went over   39

I shall die, but that is all that I shall do for Death   103

I shall forget you presently, my dear   25

I think I should have loved you presently   24

I think I will learn some beautiful language, useless for commer-
cial   122

I thought, as I wiped my eyes on the corner of my apron   142

I too beneath your moon, almighty Sex   126

I will be the gladdest thing   11

I will put Chaos into fourteen lines   153

If I should learn, in some quite casual way   14

Importuned through the mails, accosted over the telephone, over-
taken by running footsteps, caught by the sleeve, the ser-
vant of strangers   141

It came into her mind, seeing how the snow   66

It is the fashion now to wave aside   152

It's little I care what path I take   45

Let them bury your big eyes   37

Let us abandon then our gardens and go home   76

Let us be circumspect, surrounded as we are   124

Love is not all: it is not meat nor drink   86

Love me no more, now let the god depart   88

My candle burns at both ends   19

FURTHER READING

Millay's *Collected Poems* (New York: Harper & Row, 1981) are currently in print, as are her *Collected Lyrics* (1981) and *Collected Sonnets* (1988) in separate volumes. Millay's writings for the stage include several plays and an opera libretto; perhaps the most interesting of these is the one-act play *Aria da Capo* (New York: Mitchell Kennerley, 1921; also available in an acting edition from Baker's Plays, Boston). Her "Nancy Boyd" writings for *Vanity Fair* and other journals were collected in *Distressing Dialogues* (New York: Harper and Brothers, 1924) and make enjoyable 1920s-period reading. A selection of Millay's letters, edited by Allan Ross Macdougall, was published as *Letters of Edna St. Vincent Millay* (New York: Harper and Brothers, 1952). Critical writings on Millay which are still of interest today are very few, but there is some useful criticism and biographical material in Norman A. Brittin's *Edna St. Vincent Millay* (Boston: Twayne, 1982); this book also contains an excellent annotated bibliography. An authorized biography of Millay by Nancy Milford is due to be published by Random House (New York) in 1992.

ABOUT THE EDITOR

COLIN FALCK teaches modern literature at York College, Pennsylvania. His publications include two poetry collections, *Backwards into the Smoke* and *In This Dark Light;* an anthology of American and British poetry, *Poems Since 1900* (edited with Ian Hamilton); *Robinson Jeffers: Selected Poems;* and *Myth, Truth and Literature,* a critique of contemporary literary theory. He has also published poetry and criticism in many journals in the United States and in Britain.